Record and Remember

Tracing Your Roots Through

Oral History

by

Ellen Robinson Epstein

Jane Lewit

Scarborough House

Scarborough House
Lanham, MD 20706

FIRST SCARBOROUGH HOUSE EDITION 1994

Library of Congress Cataloging-in-Publication Data

Epstein, Ellen Robinson.
    Record and remember : tracing your roots through oral history /
Ellen Epstein and Jane Lewit.—1st Scarborough House ed.
        p.   cm.
    Includes bibliographical references and index.
    ISBN 0-8128-8550-3
    1. United States—Genealogy—Methodology.   2. Oral history.
I. Lewit, Jane.   II. Title.
CS14.E67   1993
929'.1'072073—dc20   93-35509
                                                                  CIP

Contents

FOREWORD   V

PREFACE   vii

1   ORAL HISTORY: A WAY TO PRESERVE THE PAST   1

2   GETTING STARTED   11

3   QUESTIONING TECHNIQUES   19

4   RESEARCHING BACKGROUND INFORMATION AND DEVELOPING AN INTERVIEW OUTLINE   29

5   RECORDING EQUIPMENT   41

6   THE INTERVIEW ITSELF: TIPS ON TAPING   51

7   INDEXING AND MAKING A GLOSSARY   61

8   TRANSCRIBING THE TAPES   67

9   ORAL HISTORY FOR CLASSROOM USE   87

10   LEGAL FORMS   101

TAPE RECORDING TERMS   105

INDEX   111

Foreword

Each of us has a story to tell. Each of us is part of a tradition. We have a rich past—and, more importantly, that past will extend into the future. Young and old will someday leave children and grandchildren who will also be part of that tradition and who will share in that history—but only if it is preserved.

This book tells you how to preserve those traditions in an exciting and creative way through what has become known as oral history—interviewing people with a past that relates to you or your interests and then recording their recollections. With Ellen Epstein and Jane Lewit as your guides you can easily become an expert amateur historian as you unearth the stories and anecdotes, the difficult times and happy times that make up your story and that will someday become part of the story of those who come after you.

One of the surprises of this venture is that you will learn that your history is more interesting than you imagined. You will learn things you never knew about. You will hear stories that even those who narrate them thought they had forgotten.

Best of all, it's fun. Creating a family or institutional history is not only interesting, it's enjoyable.

In the end, you will have a meaningful record that you and your family will treasure for generations.

Hershel Shanks
Editor, *Moment* magazine
Understanding the Dead Sea Scrolls

Preface

Record and Remember: Tracing Your Roots Through Oral History
enables you to enjoy the pleasures of being an amateur historian.
Interest in exploring the roots of individual families and institutions has never been greater. America has become disen-
chanted with the melting pot where everybody blends together
and loses their distinguishing ethnic characteristics. Today, we
believe that the national and individual interests are best served
when each group maintains its own traditions, stories, songs and
history. Oral history is the ideal way to capture and to preserve
these memories.

Record and Remember is the step-by-step guide for creating a
memorable oral history. In an extremely clear and creative way,
it teaches you how to:
  • choose the best people to interview
  • gather background information before the interview
  • ask good questions that bring forth lively anecdotes
  • purchase and use audio/video recording equipment
  • conduct the interview
  • index, edit and transcribe the interview
  • organize classroom projects on oral history
  • follow relevant oral history guidelines and legal procedures
Families, associations, community organizations, schools, and
practically any group that wants to preserve its institutional

memory will find this book useful. With *Record and Remember,* you can gain the skills and competence needed to preserve memories for posterity. The outcome is a priceless history that brings the past to life.

1

Oral History:

A Way to Preserve the Past

People love to talk, especially about themselves. Given the chance and a comfortable setting, an older person can relive earlier experiences by talking about them. Through these treasured memories, you can discover the hidden history of your family, a valued organization, or a prominent individual. A rich picture can be painted with words. In fact, the key to understanding the past may be in the anecdotes and stories told in a taped interview.

Oral history is a relatively new branch of historical research, which developed in the mid-twentieth century with the invention of the tape recorder. Technological advances in the solid-state, portable tape recorder made it possible for oral history to flourish. Originally, the purpose of oral history was to record the memoirs of famous people. Now the purpose is broader for historians recognize that everyday people have important stories to tell. Oral history is different from genealogy. In genealogy, you research a family by finding ancestors' names and dates in official archives where public records are kept. Using oral history techniques, you do not have to search far. Instead, you can gather information directly from an individual who is willing to sit with you and be interviewed.

Using a tape recorder and knowing what to ask allows you to

record and remember, to trace your own roots through oral history. The key to your past may be in the yet untold stories of an elderly relative. Asking the right questions can reveal how things used to be; who is related to whom and how; the origin of your surname or maybe your first name; family secrets or "characters"; special home remedies; the history of special heirlooms; where relatives came from and where they are buried. In the past, families kept in touch by writing letters—letters which were often carefully stored in basements or attics for future generations. Letters were a family link. Today, we pick up the phone when we want to hear the latest family news, but this process leaves no record. The tape recording of memories is the contemporary answer to written memoirs.

An oral history of an elderly relative, recorded on tape, is always available for listening. The story of how your family happened to live where it lives, have the traditions it does, perhaps even exhibit the personality or physical traits it does can be told to you on tape by a relative. It will then be available for many future generations so that they may have a better understanding of their family origins.

Oral histories are being done right now all over the country for family, scholarly, and educational purposes. You can learn how to interview your family, or start a project in your community or classroom, using a tape recorder. This will be your own search for roots and traditions—done without extensive and expensive research in libraries. The tapes can be preserved for years.

An oral history can become even more memorable and poignant once the person recorded has died. As one woman wrote:

> I received the tapes (of my father) today and have just finished listening to them. My heart aches for the opportunities I missed to learn all those things myself.
>
> As I listened to those tapes, I couldn't believe that he is really dead. He's so alive on these tapes—doing what he loved to do—talk to family and about family. And telling those wonderful stories that were always there for every occasion. That's one of

2

the things I remember thinking right after he died—what a waste—all that knowledge—all those anecdotes and stories . . .

It is possible for you to record these special family memories yourself, without laborious writing, by using a tape recorder and simple questioning techniques. Our present technology has produced relatively inexpensive tape-recording machines and cassettes that almost anyone can learn to operate. Using a tape recorder will open new opportunities to you. Aside from preserving the story of your origins as told by an elderly grandmother or grandfather, you can have the chance to talk about your own experiences for your future grandchildren. A good friend or other family member can record your stories for you. Your life story can be an inspiration for a future relative not yet born.

One of the best reasons for taping a family history is to preserve the voices of your grandparents as well as their stories and anecdotes about days past. Someday children, grandchildren or great-grandchildren may want to know their unique family history—strange places and interesting people they have vaguely heard about. Instead of putting them off with a hurried "I don't know" or repeating half-remembered stories, you now have a marvelous opportunity. A tape cassette of one of their relatives lies on the shelf ready to be played. Through the magic of technology, one captures a lost voice from the past recounting the family's history. You hear an accented voice, perhaps—with the intonations of Europe, Latin America, Asia, or even the South or Midwest of long ago. The voice of a grandmother whom your children may never have met but can feel close to by listening to her voice.

One woman, a great-grandmother who has since died, told her family tales on tape of the Civil War and of her pioneering days in South Dakota. A history book doesn't record the small acts of bravery that your family may have performed. Lenoir Hood Miller recalled:

My father enlisted in the 51st Indiana Volunteers when the Civil War broke out. He said he only had wormy bacon and

3

hard tack to eat, and he came out of the War weighing 98 pounds—a man of around 180 pounds. He just loved to tell his Civil War stories, and especially how he and his men dug their way out of Libby prison.

Libby prison was an old tobacco factory and there was a fireplace in the basement. Each night they would take out the bricks, and after weeks of working, they finally got to the place where it was safe for them to make their exit. Colonel Strait led the line, and there were three others. He was almost at the end of the line when he just couldn't make it. He was a broad-shouldered man and they hadn't made it quite wide enough. So they had to all back out. And then the next night the Colonel didn't go, but the other three did make their escape and sometime later got to the northern lines.

Though you may not trace your family roots to volunteers in the Civil War, the intricacies of your background are valuable in their own right. Bringing back memories of a parent or grand-parent can be an intensely moving experience. One middle-aged woman who listened to a tape recording of her mother admitted:

> I felt her ideals, her aspirations, her hopes, and her dreams perhaps for the first time in my forty-six years of knowing her as a "mother." My mother was my mother—and I was not separated from her—born in a shtetl, fighting tenaciously for an education, leaving Russia, adjusting to a new country, work-ing in a sweat shop at the age of fourteen, becoming an activist in the union's efforts to organize the shops, marrying, and raising her children.
>
> If for no other reason, these tapes were priceless in helping me "see" my mother as a woman, an individual I felt a great deal of love and appreciation for.
>
> I was intensely moved and emotionally involved in her story. These tapes have helped me free myself of some of the negative feelings I have had about my mother, and have helped me become much more loving and caring toward her. If for no other reason—these tapes are a gift to me.

4

When I played them for my sixteen-year old daughter, she sat mesmerized and fascinated. She listened for hours. She, too, saw and felt her grandmother in a new way and became familiar in an intensely personal way with the life in Russia and the immigrant struggle. This heritage for our children, as third-generation Americans, could not be brought more freely into their consciousness than in this moving way of hearing it in their grandparent's own voice. It is a priceless and precious and intensely personal message. The emotional impact and intellectual awareness of my mother's voice recalling memories, telling stories, laughing, crying at times, as she recounts her whole life is a most unique and precious document and a real family treasure.

The story of your family will have a sentimental value for your own relatives, but it could have historical value as well. Neighborhoods, occupations, and traditions change over the years and are forgotten. However, if a tape recording has carefully covered your family's history, it could tell the story of the way things used to be. Not only will your oral history provide pleasure for your family, it could be an important historical document.

Many immigrants to the United States have unique memories of their reactions to the strange and abundant objects in the New World. A refugee from Poland reminisced about the easy availability of fruit in America:

> We never had an orange or a lemon. Oranges and lemons would come in from Warsaw, and here [in the United States]— all these in the window! And I remember my mama had a sister in Warsaw, and they would send us in, if somebody was sick, they would send in oranges and lemons that was sort of a—you know—when you're sick—a gift.

Many families have already made tape recordings of their older relatives. In the process they have discovered history.

At the time of the voting for the Nineteenth Amendment, one woman made sure that the new immigrants marked their ballots for women's suffrage. She recalled:

And when came election time and I was too young to vote I was put down as a watcher—what you called—and watched in the places where the voting was going on. And at the time it was down on the East Side where all the peddlers would come to vote and they looked at me with . . . what is she . . . what are you doing here? And I spoke to them in Yiddish and told them, "Yeah, you put a cross here," and there were people that didn't know how to sign their name so I was able to go in with them to witness that they were putting a cross where they were supposed to put the cross. So I showed them where to put the cross for the women's vote.

One family has a story about "My Ancestor Who Didn't Fight in the Civil War." It seems that in a particular family every male descendant has been told about how a male had fought bravely in the Civil War. He had been wounded, it was said, and that was why he walked with a limp. Ever since then, it was a tradition in the family for men to serve in whatever war the United States happened to be involved in at the time. One great grandson decided to fight in Vietnam in order to preserve this family tradition. When the great-grandson returned from the war, he became interested in knowing more about his family background. As he searched oral history records, he discovered that in reality, his great-grandfather had never fought in the Civil War. This revelation may effect the lives of future male descendants in his family, for they may feel freer in choosing whether or not to enlist in wartime. Oral history allowed the great-grandson to verify his past, whatever the outcome.*

You don't need a professional oral historian to interview your family. You do need to be able to ask the right questions to elicit the responses you will require to form a memorable aural picture of your family.

All oral histories begin with origins—"Where did we come from?" "How did we get here?" "How did we earn a living?" The

---

*As told by Steve Zeitlin of the Smithsonian Institution's Family Folklife Program.

Fannie Stark Sturz with her granddaughter,
Karlyn David Robinson.
Baltimore, Maryland, c. 1923–24.

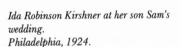

Ida Robinson Kirshner at her son Sam's
wedding.
Philadelphia, 1924.

Red Cross Volunteers during World War I
Carlisle, Pennsylvania, September 22, 1918.

job of the interviewer is to continue asking brief questions that will allow the person being interviewed to speak with little interruption and in as much detail as he or she can remember. That takes skill and practice. Questions requiring more than a one-word or one-sentence answer must be studied in advance. Nothing is more boring to listen to than "yes" and "no" answers to an interviewer's queries. Some knowledge of the family's background is absolutely essential in order to know what to ask.

Sometimes parents aren't willing to reveal certain unsavory family stories to their own children. Another family member—perhaps a grandchild or distant cousin or even a close friend—might be able to persuade reluctant relatives to speak out. Where children may be tempted to begin an oral history by asking angry or provocative questions, a less involved relative will be more likely to inquire gently.

What this book can't tell you is the value an oral history will have for your particular family. That you will have to decide for yourself. But one of the most important reasons for doing an oral history now might be to preserve your own ethnic identity.

8

A New York writer has written about her regret at not knowing why her grandparents came to America:

> It seems that I am going to have to be satisfied with a family tree that goes back to my grandparents and no further. Life for my family seems to have started on the shores of America, almost as if the family sprang out of those shores, as though everything before was nothing.
>
> But everything before wasn't nothing. Adele and Hyman in Rumania, and Fannie and Abraham in Russia, looked around and decided to take a long scary journey to something better. They were people of great courage, very different from the people who stayed to suffer. I am so sorry the story of their courage is lost to me.*

An oral history of this writer's grandparents while they were alive might have resolved some of her anguish by preserving the family immigration story.

Listening to memories from the past can serve many purposes. This experience can help bring you in touch with your family, your roots, your background. Voices on tape can help you trace how a business, an institution, a community came to be. Take the oral history now—answer questions in the present and create a record for the future.

---

*Elaine Berman, *The New York Times,* Op-Ed page, November 18, 1976.

2
Getting Started

Deciding Whom to Interview

Knowing whom to interview can assure the richest possible family history to hand on to your children. Interviewing a family member on tape can be a tremendously enriching experience. The stories told by parents about other relatives can be put into the perspective of a lifetime's events. Other stories never mentioned are often suddenly remembered when a person's life is being reviewed.

One man, an immigrant from Germany to Seguin, Texas, had always told his family that he had traveled by rail to Texas from New York. When interviewed and asked to describe the trip across the country, he dug into his memory and realized that he actually had gone from New York to Galveston by boat, and only then had taken the train to Seguin. Immigration officials had demanded a port-of-entry fee of ten dollars to disembark in New York. But the man had no money, so he stayed on the boat to its next port—Galveston.

The immigrant's family learned two important things from this oral history: how their father happened to settle in a small town in Texas, and how New York government officials deterred unwanted immigrants from entering the city.

A skillful interviewer needs to ask many questions when taping a family member. The interviewer has to choose carefully whom to interview.

It is best not to interview your own parents. A child may have an excellent relationship with his mother and father, but the child is still their child no matter how old the "child" actually is. We know of a sixty-eight year old woman who lives with her ninety-two year old mother. The mother is still complaining bitterly about her daughter's refusal to pick up the clothes in her room.

Sometimes parents cannot be completely candid with their children and it might be easier for them to open up to another person. Since a parent and child have so many mutual unspoken assumptions, it is awkward for a parent to retell specific details that he feels the child already knows. Issues between parents and children may lie beneath the surface for a lifetime. The parent may think the interview presents an opportunity to clarify family grudges. The purpose of an oral history is to find out the meaningful events in a person's life not to rehash old family feuds. A more objective, uninvolved interviewer will be able to get these stories on tape. Though it is hard to conduct a good interview with your own parent, we know one son who successfully gathered a family history from his mother and father right before their fiftieth wedding anniversary.

Often the narrator himself will try to avoid going over painful family differences in detail. They can be alluded to, but never repaired. In one case, a man being interviewed was questioned on tape, "Do you mind if I ask about your other son?" (to whom the man hadn't spoken in years). He replied:

> Look, it's useless. What good would it do? When his mother died I gave him a chance to come back into the family. . . . I only hope I live long enough 'til my grandchildren are old enough so I can see them on their own.

This family dispute was too wrenching to go over in detail. Sometimes, the person will want to give the details of a dispute. They see the interviewing session as a last chance to "clear the air" or tell their side of the story for posterity. You, the interviewer, must be sensitive to the interviewee and take your clues for questioning from there.

One good combination of interviewer and interviewee is a

grandchild interviewing a grandparent. This is true because a grandparent often has the feeling of passing down family history without the entanglements of a parent-child relationship. If a grandparent is still living, and still mentally active, then by all means go to the grandparent first. However, grandchildren in America have often moved far from their grandparents. Or, in some cases, grandparents have moved far from the Northern cities where they may have grown up, in order to live more comfortably in Southern or Western states. So there may be a problem reaching a grandparent.

Depending on how important it is to make an oral history, it may be worthwhile to write or telephone a grandparent and tell them about your oral history project. Let the grandparent know why you want to tape his or her voice and stories about the past. Who wouldn't be flattered by the attention? Who wouldn't want to be able to tell the family stories, relive the events of the past with benefit of hindsight and without the possible sufferings? And who hasn't heard of Alex Haley's success in tracing his family roots back through the past purely on the basis of family stories told by his grandmother and his cousin on their porch in Henning, Tennessee?

A grandparent may have thought about organizing his old photographs, letters, medals, and stories into some suitable form to pass on to his grandchildren. But the time necessary to do the organizing just seems to fade away. These days it's hard for people to sit down and write a long letter. Think of the strength and discipline needed to write about a lifetime's worth of stories. It's far easier for your grandparent to talk with you about his or her past. Most older people would be delighted to have the opportunity to share stories with an interested audience.

However, if a grandparent is just too far away, too frail, or not alive, there are other possibilities. This is the chance to find out more about your relatives. Determine who the best and most reliable storyteller is in the family. Everyone seems to have at least one family member who keeps the relatives entertained during reunions—or one family busybody. That's the person who might make an excellent family historian. One thing to

13

remember is that whoever is interviewed should be old enough to have lived through many historical events and young enough to remember them fairly well.

As you conduct the interview, you can accommodate to the special needs of your narrator. If the person being interviewed is hearing-impaired, consider placing yourself in clear sight so that he can take cues from your body language or read your lips. This may be important if your interviewee is elderly and hard-of-hearing. If the interview is being conducted in sign language, you will need to use a video recorder. Be sure to position the camera so that both peoples' signing can be clearly seen. Perhaps you will even want a third person using the video camera to record the interview.

Be sure to choose very carefully the person who will be the narrator. Most important is a good and accurate memory. If you are lucky, the person with the best memory may be a good storyteller as well. Some people are able to recount marvelous anecdotes when asked the simplest questions; others cannot tell a story no matter how deeply they are questioned. It is very discouraging to interview a relative who is so old and feeble that everything in the past is confused in his mind. One elderly woman whom we taped for her family could barely recall the names of her children. In order to uncover information, we were obliged to keep asking questions, most of which were answered in one word, "yes" or "no." What the family received was a tape recording which featured our questions, some very hazy phrases from the elderly woman and a mysterious outline of their family history.

One of the best interviews we have conducted involved a man named Samuel B. Lifshutz. When he was asked what the "B" in his name stood for, he launched into a very long story about how he had been mistaken for another Sam Lifshutz by a Texas bank. The other Sam Lifshutz owed a large debt to the bank, and this Sam Lifshutz was being dunned for the other man's debt. At that point, our Sam Lifshutz decided to add a middle initial, "B"—after his father, Ben—in order to differentiate himself from the Lifshutz with the bad debt.

14

All this information came from just one question, "Would you please tell me your complete name?" Sam proved to be an excellent interviewee both because he had a fine memory and because he was able to relate his memories in a very thoughtful and straightforward way.

Sam Lifshutz was an immigrant to the United States with some fascinating stories, but even people who have lived in small American towns all their lives have interesting stories to tell. It all depends on the judgment of the family interviewer—you—in choosing the family historian.

One woman who grew up in a small Midwestern town and described her life as "ordinary, plain, and simple" had some wonderful, enlightening stories to tell. This particular woman was hesitant about being interviewed because she felt she had had very few extraordinary experiences worth preserving as she had lived practically her whole life in Nikomus, Illinois. However, when she finally agreed to the oral history interview, she proved to be a sensational storyteller. Her memories of childhood games, friends, clothing, and school produced a glowing account of life in early twentieth-century America. Although her stories had little political significance, they did have historical meaning in her daily life experiences. Her "yesterdays" were deeply meaningful to her own family as history.

One of the anecdotes this woman told was especially worth remembering because of the excitement and danger that it involved to the family. The woman had never traveled abroad, but she did take trips by car across the country with her children. On one trip in the Colorado Rockies, she and her family tried to follow a shortcut on an old map. They found themselves driving up a dirt path, making hairpin turns, unable to turn back, and finally crossing Mt. Elbert by the Independence Pass, the highest point in Colorado. When they arrived, terrified and shaken, in the nearest town, Aspen, they learned that they had traveled by an old cowboy trail. It had been abandoned for years because it was too dangerous for the horses.

People may think their lives have been unexciting, but everyone has, by virtue of just living, been through important historical events that they can remember. And often the stories of their childhood are as vivid today as when they were first lived. Some of our narrators remember pioneering in the West or hearing about grandparents killed by the Indians. Their stories form a valuable recollection of American history. A sympathetic interviewer can help the stories come alive in the words of the narrator.

One elderly woman spoke about her experiences "proving up on a claim" in South Dakota. We asked her to explain what filing a claim meant, so that her great-grandchildren would know.

Well, you went to the land commissioner and he asked you questions: if you're an American citizen, and do you own any land, and do you promise to live on it for fourteen months; then he held up his hand for me to take the oath. I thought he wanted to shake hands on a good deal and I grabbed him by the hand and shook it vigorously. So we had a good laugh.

Your good choice of an interviewee will enable your children to laugh again at, and wonder about, even the most ordinary of lives. Describing how a family lived forty years ago will be of great significance in the future. Merely explaining how daily cooking was done can highlight the vast changes that American family life has undergone. Forty years ago, who would have imagined a microwave oven and its impact on household tasks? The songs that were sung to a child when he was sick in bed, recipes for cookies, weekend outings—all are as meaningful to a family as well-publicized acts of bravery. Everyone has a story to tell his family that may, in some way, be relevant to the future.

Parents can guide children in reaching most relatives, but even if a relative whom you wish to interview is no longer living, all is not lost. It is possible to produce a composite portrait of a deceased relative by interviewing people who knew him well. In one case, we achieved a composite picture of a man's father by interviewing the dead man's wife, daughter, secretary, sister, and brother. In other words, even when an important relative can no longer be interviewed, there are still memorable remnants of his life that can be reproduced on tape.

No matter whom you decide to interview, it is always best to write a letter first explaining what you intend to do. In your letter, state that you want to find out more about the history, traditions, and important events of your family, your community, your prospective interviewee's organization or business— or whatever your goal is. Your purpose is, of course, to have a permanent record on tape to hand down to future grandchildren or historians. In rare circumstances when distance or other factors prohibit a face-to-face meeting, you could try interviewing via telephone. To do this, you would need a Telephone Pick-Up device to record off the telephone.

If you choose to interview a close relative whom you've seen often while you were growing up, be sure that you can establish some psychological distance between the relative and yourself. Otherwise you may have a situation much like the parent-child relationship. A close relative could have been involved in many family feuds and not be willing to discuss certain events. Or be all too willing to discuss them—on and on and on. It may be hard to strike a balance between the too-close and too-distant relative. In that case, it's best to choose the distant relative and feel freer to ask the important questions that demand honest answers. Try to begin with the oldest person first—for obvious reasons—even though he may not be the best narrator.

Becoming a Good Interviewer
Now that you have some idea about whom to interview, it's time to think about the characteristics of a good interviewer.

The person who is to do the interviewing must be a good listener. Be sure you are able to sit back and listen to your relative talk about the family. You may not agree with what he has to say or you may have heard a different version of a certain story, but you must be able to keep quiet while your relative talks. Your job is to ask the questions that spark long responses, not to correct, elaborate, or argue. Don't jump in feet first with an angry question about some unresolved family dispute. You are trying to get an orderly oral history not a replay of family arguments. The interviewer should not use the taping session to

17

show off his knowledge of the family, his charm, his wit, his education or anything about himself. You are seeking to elicit information not to tell your own story on tape. The interviewer is like the moon; the interviewee like the sun. Remember, the moon only reflects the sun's light. If you feel you are too argumentative or really like to talk too much, choose a close friend or another family member to do the interview. In advance, you will be able to discuss the events, problems, traditions and tragedies of your family so he is prepared for a smooth interview.

The key to good recording and interviewing is following these important steps which can be learned and improved with practice:

- learning background information about the interviewee before the taping session
- preparing an outline of questions ahead of time
- setting up equipment; checking that it works properly
- keeping simple notes of names, places, and dates
- listening sympathetically and carefully to the person being interviewed; following leads in the conversation and knowing when to pursue a fruitful digression

When you finish reading *Record and Remember,* you will be well prepared to conduct an interview.

3

Questioning Techniques

People are always asking questions of each other. Sometimes they get the answers they want; sometimes they don't. Often the answer depends on the questioning technique. Vermonters are famous for avoiding precise answers to questions. One Vermont resident, when asked by a tourist, "Can I get to Newfane on this road?" replied, "If you travel further enough." What the tourist really should have asked was, "What is the fastest route to Newfane?" Then the farmer might have had a tougher time using his famous Vermont humor.

You are a tourist, too, when it comes to asking questions of your relatives. You have to travel in his mind—an uncharted territory—and you've got to learn the route. Journalists are very often experts in questioning techniques, but usually they are searching just for bare facts, not the embellishments, the anecdotes that make a person's life flavorful. Of course, you will need the bare facts, too, but your aim is to get behind the facts and develop interesting life stories.

Closed and Open-Ended Questions

There are two methods of questioning which will elicit different responses from the person being interviewed: closed questions and open-ended questions. Closed questions are easy to answer without much thinking. They usually demand a direct response and do not require a broader, philosophical reply. Closed questions are the ones journalists are most familiar with as they focus on the facts. Open-ended questions, on the other hand, are designed to let the interviewee "pick up the ball and run with it"—they call for a lengthy and thoughtful response. The open-ended question should also let you, the interviewer, shape further questions based on the interviewee's response.

You should decide whether you want an open-ended or closed response. Here are some examples of open-ended as compared to closed questions.

Samples of Open-Ended and Closed-Ended Questions for an Immigrant

Open-Ended	Closed-Ended
1. How was daily home life in the old country different from your home life here?	1. What was the name of the town where you were born?
2. What were the conditions on the boat (plane, etc.) coming to the United States?	2. How did you come to the United States?
3. Tell me about any unusual or different things that you saw when you first arrived here.	3. What was the first thing you saw when you arrived here?
4. Why did you choose ____ town to live in when you came to the United States?	4. What town did you settle in when you came to the United States?
5. How were you treated by your neighbors here?	5. Were you treated badly or well by your new neighbors?
6. Why did you choose the job you took when you arrived here?	6. Where did you begin to work in the United States?
7. How did your religious practices differ in the old country from those in the United States?	7. Did religion play an important part in your lives?

20

Questions that you might want to ask a non-immigrant may be slightly different:

Open-Ended Compared to Closed-Ended Questions for a Non-immigrant

Open-Ended	*Closed*
1. What do you remember about the town where you were born?	1. Where were you born?
2. What kind of stories did your parents or grandparents tell you about where they were born?	2. Where were your parents born?
3. How did you "prove up on a claim"?	3. Did many young people move west alone to "prove up on a claim"?
4. How was your family affected by the Second World War?	4. Did any members of your family serve in the Second World War?
5. Why did you end your schooling?	5. When did you end your schooling?
6. What were family reunions like?	6. Did your family get together for reunions?
7. What were your feelings about presidential elections when you first voted?	7. When did you first vote?

As you can see, more is demanded of the interviewee when he answers an open-ended question. However, much more is demanded of you, too, and therefore you might want to practice formulating questions in your mind before conducting the interview. During the interview you may become too self-conscious if you are constantly trying to think of open-ended compared to

21

closed questions. You need the time during the interview to concentrate on the interviewee. As you go over your background information before the interview, try to develop some key questions that might call for lengthy responses.

Also, when you formulate an open-ended question, be careful not to make it too broad. Most of us are familiar enough with friends who ask, "How was your trip?" What can you answer to a question like that? It practically cries out for a one-word response like "great" or "fine." The question is really just being polite rather than asking a probing question. You are not interested in a polite, conventional response during a taping session. Instead of asking "How was your trip?", you might focus on specific aspects of the trip. "What were some of the outstanding restaurants on your trip?" or "Tell me about some of the people you met in _____ ?" will probably command useful and descriptive answers from your friends.

Best of all is a combination of closed and open-ended questions. Begin with a closed question in order to establish a basic fact. Then ask open-ended questions which should enhance the fact with personal meaning.

For instance, to find out about the way certain family holidays were celebrated, you might ask, "What holiday was particularly important to your family?" Then follow up with, "What are some of the traditions you remember about that holiday?" or "Tell me about the foods you ate on that day, the songs you sang, or who gathered together on these occasions." Hopefully, you will receive a full picture of special family celebrations by asking well-rounded questions.

Using the technique of asking open-ended questions, we asked one interviewee several follow-up questions to the closed question: "Where did you go to college?" What we received was not only the name of the college, but also an entire history of what people thought of women's education in the early 1900's and how the interviewee felt about attending a well-known Ivy League school:

> At the age of twelve, my father took us into New York for a treat, and I saw *Daddy Longlegs,* which is a story written about

22

Vassar. And I decided that I would go to Vassar—so I worked and I studied and I tried to get high marks, and I did. They told my father he was a fool. Why spend money on a girl to send her to college? He was willing—we were all gung-ho on education. That was what mattered. You scrimped and saved and you did everything to get a total education. And I got a scholarship and I went to Vassar and I never considered any other college.

In another interview, we had been told to ask about a former slave who became a family friend. The interviewee knew that we were familiar with the story, and we were having a difficult time persuading the storyteller to repeat the famous anecdote. We first asked, "Do you have a story about 'Mammy Julie'?" But the interviewee just gave the background of where "Mammy Julie" lived, not the story that was wanted. Once more, we asked, "What exactly happened with her? What's the exact story?" The interviewee was still reluctant and replied, "Well, you see—I don't remember anything about it. It was only hearsay that I heard." We persisted. "Well, can you tell me the story?" Finally, the interviewee agreed to read a letter from her cousin about "Mammy Julie" . . .

Whether her name was "Mammy Julie" or not I don't remember—she just speaks of her as Mammy. She said, "Our grandfather bought a little seven-year-old girl slave and she was raised with his eleven children. When she was a young woman, this was right after the [Civil] War, she lived with them anyhow because she couldn't read or couldn't write. When she was a young woman, Grandma taught her housework and cooking (or the house servants did), then one day Grandpa heard that some of her relatives were nearby across the river. So they asked her if she would like to go visit them. Of course she said yes. They had her driven to where they were. They immediately had her married to one of them and she gave birth to a boy—Sam. His name was really Sambo, they called him Sam at that time.

"When she was gone a year, the children wanted her back.

23

They all loved her so. One day my mother took a horse and rode across the river to where she was, and said, 'Mammy—I've come for you.' Took the baby and rode off with him, knowing how his mother would follow because he had to be fed, and which of course she did.

"The next day her husband came demanding that she go back with him. She refused, telling him that this was her home and her folks. The children all armed themselves with brooms and canes and threatened if he did not leave, threatened him if he would take her.

Mammy was like a grandma to me. Sam, the son, was a loving brother. So when grandma passed on, mother inherited Mammy and Sam who lived out their lives in our home."

This was an important and special family story that would have been lost if we had not been both persistent and careful. We continued to ask for the entire story about "Mammy Julie" rather than to ask single, closed questions like, "Did 'Mammy Julie' live with your family?" which would have ruined the continuity of the anecdote.

Sometimes, no matter how adroit you are at asking questions, the narrator is unable to answer in as complete a way as you would desire. People have different methods of telling stories, and some interviewees just aren't able to spin a tale in an interesting manner. We have examples of this difficulty from two separate occasions. Both interviewees were asked the same question: "Can you describe the home you grew up in?" The answers reflect both the personality and storytelling ability of each narrator. The first narrator answered:

As I told you, it [the home] was on the corner, with seven big display windows. The store was downstairs, and we lived on the first floor, which was later taken over by the store which was an extra addition in back.

The second narrator answered like this:

It was a pretty good house, yes, it was concrete, built of concrete. You know, cement floors. And there was something

24

very unusual. How do you call it? Underneath you'd put straw. You warm it and then you sleep on it like a bed or a couch.

Question: "What was it called?

Answer: "Let's see. My, my, my—*Gelangi* [a Russian word]. It would heat the whole house."

Question: "Who would sleep there?"

Answer: "At night you slept on it. It was built on concrete. A very wide space. Four or five people could sleep on it."

Question: "Did you and your brothers sleep there?"

Answer: "Yes, then we had two beds, my father and mother slept in the bed. Then we had another bed. Then we had the Gelangi—a very wide space that kept warm. We only used it at winter time when it was real cold—real cold."

Question: "What was the rest of the house like? A separate dining room like we know it today?"

Answer: "Yes, a separate room with chairs and tables. We didn't have nothing fancy. The stove was made of concrete and we used to bake our own bread. We used wood and straw for heating—winter time in the oven we used wood but the place where we used to sleep [the Gelangi] we used straw."

The narrator of the first story remembered his home, but he either wasn't able to project warmth and details of his childhood or he preferred not to. On the other hand, the second interviewee spoke with happiness about an obviously fondly remembered childhood home. The question was the same, but the narrators responded to it in entirely different ways.

A final tip about questioning techniques—ask only one question at a time. A long series of questions is not only confusing but also impossible to answer. What you will probably get is an answer to the first or last question in the series or a request to repeat the question, something you might not be able to do. Keep it brief. Ask clear-cut questions that will allow the speaker to slide effortlessly into his remembrances of things past.

Jerome Epstein, immigrant from Mariampole, Lithuania. Photo c. 1930, taken in San Antonio, Texas, to send back to his parents in Europe.

A Sunday outing in Poland, c. 1920.

Samuel Rau
Trenton, New Jersey, c. 1900.

Mira Leah Rau
Trenton, New Jersey, c. 1900.

27

Epstein family portrait
Mariampole, Lithuania, c. 1920.

4

Researching Background Information and Developing an Interview Outline

Researching Background Information on the Interviewee
Once you have settled on the right person to interview, you will want to find out as much as you can about this person. Walking into an interview unprepared is foolish. Not only are you unsure of what you are doing, but you will not even know the right questions to ask.

Tell your interviewee exactly what you intend to do and that your goal is an oral history tape. You have chosen him for he has a wealth of information. Your next step is to ask for background material. You can call or write your prospective interviewee to ask whether he has any photographs, news clippings, old letters, or other material about the family. Try not to get him involved in extensive reminiscences that you will want included in your oral history tapes. Otherwise, at the actual interview, you may ask a question and your interviewee's reply will be, "I told you that story last week on the phone."

If your interviewee does send you some important material, be sure to read it carefully in order to prepare the questions you will want to ask during the interview. If there is too much

29

material for your relative to collect, you might decide to do it yourself. If your relative lives close by that presents no problem. If not, a friend or relative who lives near the interviewee might be willing to cull the material for you. However, don't count on it. A special trip to your relative just to review the material is not suggested, basically because the relative may decide then and there to talk to you—and you will be unprepared. The best stories may be revealed at that time, never to be retold or to lose spontaneity told the second time around. It is far better to rely on other methods of discovery.

If there is too little material available—no family records, photographs without names, misplaced family bibles and letters—you might try locating birth, death, and marriage certificates for specific dates. The United States Government Printing Office, Superintendent of Documents, Washington, D.C. 20402, has booklets which tell you where to write for birth and death certificates, divorce records, and marriage certificates. However, may be easier just to begin interviewing with relatively little information but with a knowledge of how to ask pertinent questions. You can retrieve a wealth of information in one good interview.

You never know where important family information may come from. One family found a poem which gave important background facts that an interviewer might have spent endless hours trying to uncover.

Why We Are in America

My mother and father lived in Russia
They owned a home and store and they fumbled along
And they had eight children.
And their thoughts were always directed to the question how to
    make a living.
The name of the oldest son was Aaron.
He wanted to lavish money like a baron.
At age fourteen he went away to work
To sell sacks of salt for someone else.
He worked for him four years

30

But his work did not progress toward higher wages,
His parents began to consider
Perhaps to send him to America to Uncle Ben
Who at that time lived in Chicago
And with whom they had some contact.
So he traveled to America
Before he became eighteen.
And his father pawned
His golden watch for an interest-free loan
In order to have money for a ship ticket and clothing.
And when he had been in America two months
He wrote to his brother Berchik
That here they live like magnates.
For that reason he should come right away
Because it is ideal here for a watchmaker.
And this was in 1913
When brother Meyer was nineteen.
He had grown up small and thin, with a pair of large eyes
And he had become suitable for working in father's store.
Both brothers wrote from America
(Although they exaggerated about many things)
That he should leave Russia as soon as possible
Because if he stayed there he would be making a mistake.
And they sent him a second-class ship ticket
And he departed immediately, he wasn't crazy.
And three weeks later he arrived at their place.
They took him to night school right away.
Brother Aaron (who was called Harry here)
Threatened him that if he remained a greenhorn
He could only become a servant to someone else.
And since Meyer had worked
Quite some time in Uncle Ben's store
He was, as they say in America, "all right"
Because he understood the English language
And he wanted to go into business for himself.
He went out with brother Harry to sell for themselves
And they quickly earned a few dollars from it.

They used to send money to mother and father
So that they could afford a festive meal even in the middle of the
*week.**

Be sure to tell your relatives why they are being questioned so closely. While you may seek to be persuasive, never appear intimidating. They may have quite different and even sinister explanations about your investigation. Perhaps you have found out something unsavory about a relative and want to publicize it. Nothing will close relationships faster than that. Or maybe you are looking for a secret inheritance. Who knows what relatives will think if you don't tell them directly what you are doing? Be very candid in all your phone calls and letters. Try to explain the purpose of oral history and your interest in preserving your unique family stories.

The kind of background information you want often depends on the person you will be interviewing and the kind of history you are aiming for. If you will be interviewing an older, feeble person, you'll want to stick close to the chronological facts of his life and try to fill in with as many stories as he remembers. If you are taping a younger, stronger individual, the chronological facts will only form an outline to what will hopefully be a series of anecdotes about the family. Sometimes you may want to limit the history to the family business or the recollections of a famous relative and his influence on history.

You will want to know in advance certain basic facts about the interviewee even though you will be asking the same questions on tape. It helps you to ask more searching questions during the interview if you know background details.

Factual Data to be Gathered in Advance,
if Possible

About Relatives	About Business
1. Full name	1. What is the business?
2. Date and place of birth	2. Who were the founders?

*By Yudie Epstein, December 22, 1939. Translated from the Yiddish by J. Michael Stern.

32

About Relatives	*About Business*
3. Places where grew up	3. When did it start?
4. Education	4. How did it start?
5. Marriage and spouse's family	5. Various locations of the business
6. Children, names of	6. Growth of business—changes of name, changes of personnel
7. Military service	7. Problems—with employees, debts
8. Occupation	8. Present state of business
9. Interests and hobbies	
10. Verify family traditions and stories you may have heard	
11. Ask for family recipes, jokes, songs, expressions	

In advance, try to collect as much material as possible. You will feel far more confident while conducting the interview, and your interviewee will be impressed that you have taken the time to learn something about his or her life experience.

Advice on Outlining

When you have gathered as much information as you can about the person to be interviewed, it is a good idea to write a general outline of the subjects you'll want to cover during the interview. Naturally, you will be getting most of your information by asking questions. However, when you plan your general outline, it is not a good idea to word the exact question you want to ask. It is far too restricting to tie yourself down to specific questions. That is why an outline, using the background information you have available, will let you be flexible during an interview. Your outline will allow you to guide the interview slightly, but it should also provide the opportunity to let the interviewee "fill in the blanks."

Although some may disagree, our experience has shown that it is best not to provide the interviewee with a questionnaire either in advance of your taping the session or at the session, for two reasons:

• The interviewee may prepare "canned answers" to your questions and you will not get the spontaneous response you want.

• The interviewee may feel that the interview is more than he or she can handle—he or she can't possibly remember that much and may decide to call the whole thing off.

Sample Outlines for the Interview

Here are three suggested interview outlines. Personalize your outline by adding pertinent background information that you have collected. Specific names and details will help you focus the interview. We suggest that you leave lots of white space in the margin of your outline so that you can jot down additional notes during the interview.

Suggested Outline of an Interview with an Immigrant

I.   Name
  1.   Where and when born
  2.   Names of paternal and maternal great-grandparents and grandparents. Description of ancestors. Interests. Physical traits. Occupations. Same for grandparents
II. The Old Country
  1.   Conditions of life: typical day—how spent
  2.   Description of the home; siblings; holidays
  3.   Description of the town: the main street
III. Circumstances surrounding decision to leave old country
  1.   Political reasons
  2.   Poverty
  3.   Religious ideas
  4.   Military conscription

5. Memories of farewells: packing up
6. Port of departure
7. Trip from hometown to port
8. Anecdotes, misfortunes
IV. The trip to America
   1. Specific incidents: conditions aboard boat; length of journey; name of ship; friends made
   2. Fears about America
V. Where landed in America
   1. First memories of objects or people in the United States
   2. The immigration process at Ellis Island or other port of entry
VI. From port of entry to final destination
   1. Why settled in certain town
   2. How traveled to destination
   3. Anecdotes; miscellaneous comments

Suggested Outline for Non-immigrant Interviewee

I. Name
   1. Where and when born
II. Background of family
   1. Where from
   2. Names of maternal and paternal great-grandparents (or further back); grandparents; parents; descriptions; physical traits
   3. Why settled in present location
   4. Occupations of ancestors
   5. Any stories, traditions, observances, recipes, objects passed on from old country
   6. Relations with neighbors who might be from different ethnic group

After determining whether your interviewee is an immigrant or not, then continue with the general Outline of Family History.

Sample Outline of Family History

I.   GREAT GRANDPARENTS (OR GRANDPARENTS)

Paternal Side: Great Grandfather:

Name; who named for

Where and when born (which generation
    came to America; how and why; describe)

Physical description

Interests

Occupation

Memories of time spent together

Any object that he gave you or that you may
    have that belonged to him

When and how died

Where buried

Anecdotes or special stories about

Great Grandmother: Same as above

Add any special recipes

Home remedies she may have used

Her interests

Date of death; burial place

Maternal Side: Great Grandfather:

Name

Where and when born; (which generation
    came to America; how; why; describe)

Physical description

Interests

Occupation

Memories of time spent together

Any object that he gave you or that you may
    have that belonged to him

When and how died

Where buried

Anecdotes or special stories

Great Grandmother: Same as above

Add any special recipes

Home remedies she may have used

Her interests
Date of death; burial place

II.   GRANDPARENTS:

                  Same as above.

Paternal Side: Grandfather

                  Grandmother

Maternal Side: Grandfather

                  Grandmother

III. PARENTS:

Father: Name; who named for
Where and When born; which generation
     came to America; describe circumstances
Occupation
Interests
Personality
His Siblings: describe each in detail with their
     spouses and children; where live
Special memories of
Problems with
Memories of special events
His date of death; where buried

Mother: Name; who named for
Where and when born; which generation
     came to America; describe circumstances
Occupation
Interests
Personality
Her siblings: describe each in detail with their
     spouses and children; where live
Special memories of
Problems with
Memories of special events
Her date of death; where buried

IV. SIBLINGS OF INTERVIEWEE

Names of each
Childhood memories of

37

Who they married
Their children
Relationship with each
Any serious illnesses

IV.   EARLY YEARS:

Schooling: Secular and/or religious
(Cover each topic separately)

Favorite teachers
Best subjects
Special friends

After school duties/chores/activities/games in
the street

V.   BEGINNINGS OF HIS/HER CAREER

College-courses; where; friends; interests;
activities
Graduate work
How chose his field
Earliest job
Mentors
Problems
Any discrimination from others
Special memories
Advice to those entering the field today

VI.   COURTSHIP AND MARRIAGE:

How met
How long courted; where and when gave
engagement ring
Where and when married
Honeymoon
His/her parents: describe each in detail
His/her siblings
Special events in their marriage

VII.   CHILDREN:

Birth of
Memories of
Summers
Camps
Vacations together

VIII. DEATH OF SPOUSE
>> Dates; details; where buried

IX. BIRTH OF GRANDCHILDREN
>> Names; dates; special message to each
>> individually

X. CURRENT INTERESTS AND ACTIVITIES

XI. MESSAGE TO GRANDCHILD; PHILOSOPHY OF LIFE
>> (If not already covered in the course of the
>> interview.)

ADDITIONAL NOTES:

The basic outline may look like a tremendous amount of territory to cover. But we encourage you to acquire as much detail as possible from your narrator. Remember, the object of the oral history is to hand down taped reminiscences and recollections to your children and grandchildren, your social club or organization, your business associates, or your town or community.

5

Recording Equipment: Tape Recorders, Video Cameras, Other Equipment You Need for Your Project

Tape Recorders

Tape recorders are perfect for oral history purposes. The equipment is relatively inexpensive and extremely easy to operate. Portable tape recorders are reliable, light weight and compact. They fit easily on a coffee table or a desktop while you are interviewing. There are choices in models and accessories depending on how much you wish to spend and the degree of quality you wish to attain.

The range upward in price from $25. In choosing one, look for ease of operation—the fewer controls and gadgets to adjust the better. Consider your needs, because the most expensive machine may not be suited to your purposes. You may be familiar with the Sony Walkman and its clones which have developed primarily for listening. However, most of these machines do not have the capability of recording. When you are shopping, you are looking for the full size cassette recorder.

Here are BASIC FEATURES to look for in choosing a machine:

• AN A.C. ADAPTER CORD—Used as the main source of power for the tape recorder. Batteries should only be used as a last resort because they are unreliable.

• EASY TO OPERATE MAIN SWITCHES—It is desirable to have all switches latch in place so that you need not keep your fingers on the fast forward or rewind buttons when operating the machine.

• AN EXTERNAL MICROPHONE—If you can find one which comes with an external mike, this is preferable.

Be careful when choosing an external microphone. To function properly, most of these need a button cell battery. There are two kinds of external mikes, one which you place on a table and one which you clip to your clothing. The external mike which sits on a table costs about $100.00. Check that it has its own stand so that it can be propped at an angle rather than lying flat on the table. When choosing this mike, be sure to get an "omni-directional" mike as opposed to a "uni-directional" one. The omni-directional mike will pick up all voices within a three foot radius. This is particularly useful for a two person interview. The uni-directional is not suitable for taking an oral history for it must be held close to the speaker's mouth and would therefore have to be transferred from person to person each time someone begins to speak. Be sure to take your machine with you for microphones and recorders must have matching plugs and receptacles. There is also a factor called "impedance" which determines whether a particular mike will work with a specific machine.

Your other choice for an external mike is the lavalier which is pinned directly to your clothing. This is most commonly used on television talk shows. For this type of mike, both you and the interviewee need to have your own, individual microphones. You will also need a "Y" cord which enables each microphone to be plugged in to the spurs of the "Y." The bottom, single line of the "Y" plugs into the machine transmitting the sound through

42

the single feeder. These mikes cost approximately $35.00 each and the "Y" cord about $5.00.

All standard-size tape recorders come with a built-in internal microphone. If you do not wish to get involved with extra equipment, you can always stick with your internal mike. The internal microphone can be noisier for it picks up the sound of the tape turning in the machine. However, it would produce a satisfactory oral history.

• AUTOMATIC LEVEL CONTROL—an internal, self-regulating adjustment that permits the machine to record different voice levels without regulating the volume control.

• BATTERY INDICATOR/RECORDING LEVEL METER—A small window with a needle which jumps to show whether the batteries are functioning and whether voices are being recorded.

Here are some OPTIONS to consider:

• DIGITAL TAPE COUNTER—Measures revolution of the tape and enables you to see how much tape remains. While some people find it helpful, most experts have found it not to be reliable for the counter varies and the tape stretches over many uses.

• TAPE REVERSING SWITCH—A convenient mechanism which allows playing the opposite side of the cassette without removing it from the machine. Available on some machines. But an electronics expert warns that it is "an encumbering thing that is likely to break down."

• PAUSE CONTROL—Enables you to stop the machine temporarily without creating a slag or click on the tape.

• FOOT PEDAL—Attachment that plugs into the machine opening marked *remote control* and enables you to operate the machine with your foot instead of your hand. Useful only for transcribing purposes.

• DUMMY MICROPHONE PLUG—A short, stubby object that is supplied with some machines and plugs into *mic* outlet. It lets you erase a portion of the cassette tape when you simultaneously push down the *play* and *record* buttons. If you make a simple mistake in recording your introduction, you can wipe the phrase out with the dummy microphone plug and record cor-

43

rectly. (Or you can simply record over your mistake by beginning again.)

• HEADSET AND SINGLE EARPHONE—Many machines come with a single earphone which enables you to listen to the tape privately, but it is very uncomfortable to use it for long periods of time. A headset, or earphone that looks like earmuffs, offers an easier way to listen to the tapes, especially for a historian who listens to many tapes.

• DEMAGNETIZER—Looks like a magic wand and is used to neutralize magnetic particles from the recording head located in the machine itself. Magnetic tape contains magnetizable iron oxide particles which coalesce when voice imprints are recorded. After many hours of use, some magnetic particles will rub off onto the recording head. These invisible magnetic particles collect on the head and interfere with clear tape recording. A demagnetizer should be used after approximately twenty hours of recording.

RECOMMENDED TAPE RECORDERS

Low Priced Machines
Cost $30.–$50. Generally available in discount department stores. All come with an AC cord; no external microphone.

SONY TCM 818
PANASONIC RQ 2102
GENERAL ELECTRIC AC 35025 S

Mid-Priced Machines
Cost $60.00–$120.00. May be found in specialized electronics stores.

PANASONIC RQL 335: Has an a/c cord and a built-in mike with adjustable sensitivity; "Walkman" size.

AIWA HSJ470: Also "Walkman" sized; contains a radio; does not come with an a/c cord but an adapter can be purchased; has no internal mike but has an external, stereo mike; may be more suitable for recording music than oral history.

Recording Equipment

Expensive Machines

Cost $250.00–$600.00. Found in specialized electronics stores or through catalogues such as J & R Music World at (800) 221-8180.

SONY TCS 2000 or TCM 5000 EV—Both are excellent machines which are often used by journalists; they have many features that assure an excellent quality recording.

MURANTZ PMD 201, PMD 221, PMD 420 or PMD 430: Superb machines; the first two models are mon-aural, the second two, stereo; a/c cords, durable cases for travelling, excellent sound quality; vu meters, automatic level control, and many other desirable features.

The SONY tape recorders can take an external microphone (Model ECM 909). This stereo, omni-directional mike requires a battery and comes with its own stand. The current price is approximately $100.00.

For lavalier mikes, check for model ECM 144 or ECM 155. The ECM 144 currently costs $50.00, while the ECM 155 costs $80.00. Remember you will need two of whichever model you select.

Video Cameras

People frequently ask why we emphasize cassette recorders over video cameras for taking an oral history. We find it easier to use a tape recorder for these purposes, because you can conduct the interview while taping inobtrusively. If you use video equipment, you lose the psychological intimacy of the interview for the video camera's presence or the presence of a third person operating the camera can be intimidating. If you choose to use video equipment, we suggest you set up the camera on a tripod behind you and focus directly on the interviewee. You can buy a hand-held remote switch to activate the camera once you have sat down to begin interviewing. Then you will have a minimal amount of disruption from your mechanical equipment.

Since one oral history can run as long as six to twelve hours, you may feel that watching someone speak for that length of time can detract from the finished product. If one only sees the person speaking, this is known in the video industry as a "talking head." It can produce a boring outcome. On the other hand, if you have the technical capacity to add visuals, such as maps, photographs, and family trees, then the video may be the preferred method of taping.

There are two types of video recorders. The 8 mm recorders are generally lighter weight, more portable and may fit in the palm of your hand. These recorders use a smaller tape which cannot be directly inserted into a VCR. This type of tape can only be played directly through the television, after hooking up the camera to the back of the set. When you do this, there is some visual distortion. If you have this machine and wish to convert the tape to a standard VHS cassette, check the Yellow Pages to find a business which makes this conversion. The other type of video camera is called VHS. Its cassette is identical in size to a standard video and can be inserted directly into a VCR. Since this field is ever-changing, we suggest that you get up-to-the-minute advice on the newest technology. When buying any video equipment, the following should be included: battery pack, charger, carrying case, a/c adapter.

Suggested Video Cameras
- 8 mm CAMERAS—price range $550.–$1100.
  Magnavox
  RCA P-0807
  GE 8 mm C 6812
  Canon 8 H 800
  Sony TR-9
  Sony CCDFX 410
  Sony TR—81
- VHS—price range $600–$1500.
  Panasonic PV 42
  Sharp VLL 30
  Magnavox CVN 322

46

G.E. HQ VHS
JVC GRM 7 PRO
JVC GR 8AM 4U

Tripods can range in cost from $80.–$200. A better quality tripod typically has a mount which is adjustable to fit your particular camera.

Regular video tapes run from 120–130 minutes. Brands such as Sony, Fuji, and Scotch are quite similar in price, ranging from 3/$10.00 to 5/$15.00. Do not buy compact video tapes for they are not suitable for this project.

Cassettes

Standard cassette tapes are available in four different playing times—designated C-30, C-60, C-90, and C-120. The number indicates the minutes of playing time for two sides of tape; therefore each side has a recording time equal to one-half the listed time. Since all cassette tapes are run at a constant speed (1⅞ inches per second), the tape is thinned out in order to achieve a longer playing time. The thinner the tape, however, the more likely it is to tangle and jam. We recommend that you buy C-60 or C-90 cassettes because they are the most durable. Remember that the C-60 will play for 30 minutes on a side while the C-90 goes for 45 minutes. So be aware when you may be running out of tape, so that you can flip the tape at a convenient time. Note that there are micro-cassettes on the market which are primarily used for dictating and answering machines, but are not adequate for oral history purposes. The thirty minute per side time also makes it simpler to check your watch or clock when you are conducting an interview.

Although there are many cheap blank tapes on the market, we don't advise buying them. Most brand-name tapes, such as Fuji, TDK, Scotch, Sony, and Maxell, cost about $2.00 and are well worth the price. They provide quality and are less liable to twist or record sound unevenly. You don't need to purchase "high fidelity" type tapes, which are too sensitive for voice recording. Low noise tapes do just fine.

In the unlikely event that your tape becomes tangled or unglued from one of the reels, cassette cases which are secured with five Phillips screws instead of glued together, can be opened easily. Then you stand a chance of repairing the tape without gouging the case and causing additional damage.

After you finish the interview, in order to avoid re-recording on your completed tape, use a ballpoint pen to punch in the two tabs located at the top of the cassette case. Punching the tabs makes it impossible for the recording head to make contact with the tape. Ideally, you should make a duplicate copy of your complete interview for safekeeping.

A few words about storing your tapes . . . A good cassette tape is practically indestructible. Tape is not only enclosed in its own solid container, but most are sold in hard plastic cases which can be reused for storage. The cassettes should always be replaced in their original plastic containers and then stored on edge, like a book. Some cassette boxes are cardboard and not made for permanent storage. Be sure to look for outer cases that have two spindles which slip through the openings in the cassette reels and secure the tape with adequate and even tension. Carrying cases that can hold a number of tapes in a book-like folder are also available.

It is best to store a tape in a closet or bureau drawer in your home—not in an unheated attic or basement. Dust, cold, and heat will affect the plastic tape, changing the quality of sound. If the tapes have been exposed to extreme temperatures, they should be allowed to return to normal room temperature (55–75 degrees) gradually. Allow sixteen to twenty-four hours for the tapes to adjust before using.

Naturally, you may be concerned about accidental erasures of the tape. This cannot occur when you are listening to the tape, especially if you have broken out the two tape tabs. However, erasure can occur by exposure to extreme heat (above 120 degrees) or to relatively strong magnetic fields. It is hardly likely that any strong sources of magnetism will be found in your home. Keeping the tapes as little as six inches away from electric transformers and motors will protect them. And even X-rays do not appear to endanger the tapes, although X-ray equipment could affect them if the tapes are stored too close to the machinery. Airline officials also assure us that X-rays which might be encountered in airport security equipment will not damage the tapes. However, magnetic door latches, such as those found on kitchen cabinets, can cause tape erasures. Do not store tapes near magnetic latches or children's toys containing magnets.

Supplies to Bring on an Interview

You will need the following equipment for an interview:

Extra cassettes—more than you think you will need
Extra batteries—if you absolutely must record with batteries
Two extension cords, at least fifteen feet long, for the machine (sometimes a wall outlet is far from a table)
Scarf, handkerchief, or towel to fold over the external microphone in order to muffle extraneous noise or to place under a mike so it doesn't sit directly on a hard wooden table.
Pencils
Pad of paper to take notes during the interview
Your outline or questionnaire
A watch or clock (if it doesn't tick too loudly) for timing the cassette

Bring these along with the tape recorder to minimize any chance of losing the interview for lack of proper equipment.

Maintenance of the Machine

Cassette tape recorders are generally well-encased and rugged. They require a minimum of maintenance as does the cassette itself. Treat the recorder and cassettes with care. Never take a tape recorder to the beach, for instance, because the sand and the moisture can penetrate the machine and rust the parts. Dust, tobacco, food, and water are all to be kept away from the machine. Batteries should be removed when not in use. The chemicals in the batteries can leak out and can ruin your machine. Before replacing them in your machine, use a battery tester to make sure that they are functioning properly.

To clean the tape recorder, remove the cassette and look for the *head*—a small projection which engages the cassette to the machine. This head should be cleaned with a cotton swab only, never with an abrasive or metal object. Wipe alcohol on the head to remove any oxide debris or lint. It will look polished and shiny when clean. You could also clean the heads on your machine with a cassette and liquid cleaner designed especially for this purpose. These packages are readily available and inexpensive.

After using the tape recorder for twenty hours, you should demagnetize the recording head. Even though nothing is visible, magnetic particles are transferred from the tape to the head. A demagnetizer will neutralize these particles.

Following these simple precautions will produce a clear recording.

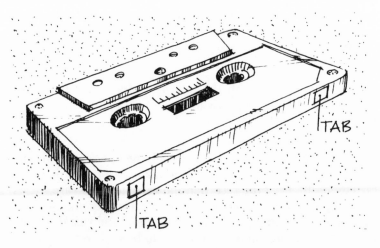

Enclosed cassette tape showing the two tape tabs to be punched out in order to prevent re-recording or erasure of the tape.

6

The Interview Itself:
Tips on Taping

Setting Up the Interview

Having chosen a family member to interview, researched background on the person, familiarized yourself with questioning techniques and your tape-recording machine, and written up a general outline of topics to be covered, you are now ready to tape the interview itself. Since you will have already alerted your relative to your purpose in interviewing him, all you need do in advance is to make an appointment for the interview, telling the interviewee to allow at least two hours for the taping session. The interviewee should be alone with you for the recording period. You can establish a more comfortable rapport in a one-to-one relationship, and besides, your purpose is to get one story, not a debate between family members. Stress this, politely, to the interviewee if he asks to have another relative present during the interview. Be firm about discouraging onlookers. You don't want interruptions and contradictions.

Before you leave for the interview, be sure your tape recorder is in good working condition—the record head of the machine cleaned with a cotton-tipped swab and alcohol, and all your equipment and supplies in an easily accessible place such as a carrying bag.

You should do the interview at the home of your relative, not at your home if you can avoid it. The reason for this is to make the interviewee as comfortable as possible. He or she will be talking for a long time, and it helps to be in a favorite chair in familiar surroundings. For the very same reason, you need to be alert when you position yourself for the interview. Be aware of the most comfortable seat in the room, and don't sit in it. Let your narrator choose where he or she would like to sit first. Also, tell the interviewee that since he will be relating a connected history for a certain length of time, the fewer the interruptions by phone or visitors, the better. Keep dogs, cats, and other animals out of the room, too, since the tape recorder will pick up every extraneous noise in the room.

Before you begin the interview, you will want to check on other things in the room to be sure they don't interfere with the recording:

1. To cut down on superfluous noise, close the windows and doors (if this doesn't make the room too stuffy). Dogs barking, children playing, airplanes overhead, clocks, air conditioners, fluorescent lights—all will leave an electronic imprint you don't want on the tape. In an office building, you can usually turn the room fan (air conditioner fan) off. Don't unnecessarily antagonize an interviewee by insisting that all noise be removed. One of our interviewees had a grandfather clock that faithfully chimed every fifteen minutes. The narrator felt very strongly that the chimes should be left on the tape, explaining that her husband had given her the clock as a wedding present sixty-five years ago, and that a day had not passed without her hearing these chimes.

   Also, the sounds of people coming downstairs, running in the halls, and washing dishes can all be picked up by the machine. But don't become overanxious about this, as some noises are inevitable.

2. Other electronic equipment in the room or nearby can scramble the recording by affecting the magnetic signals received on tape. Try not to record near an air conditioner or elevator. Of course, no background music, no matter how soothing, should be playing during the taping session.

52

3. Check whether flourescent lights in the room are buzzing. This noise will be picked up as you record.
4. Some electrical sockets pick up radio stations. We once interviewed in a home library where one outlet picked up a local radio station and transmitted the voices on to the tape. Fortunately, when we moved the plug to another outlet in the same room, this was not a problem.

Some noises can't be done away with. The manner in which people speak often includes involuntary thumpings with the fist for emphasis, clapping hands, and shifting position in the chair. One man banged his hand on a nearby table each time he finished telling a good anecdote. The sound on the tape rolls in like thunder. There isn't much you can do to prevent this without hampering a person's style and making him feel self-conscious. However, persistent noises can be noted in the typed transcript of the tape, e.g., ". . . at several points on the tape extraneous sounds can be heard. The most obvious is the sound of the interviewee banging his fist on the table for emphasis."

After checking to remove whatever noisemakers you can, you will want to set up your equipment. A good seating arrangement would be to have a table between you and the narrator so that you can place the microphone and the tape recorder on the table. If you can leave a little space between the mike and the machine, this would be desirable. Some of the mechanical noises that fill the air can be muffled by putting the mike on top of a folded towel. This will not interfere with voice recording.

On any hard surface be sure to cushion the microphone with the towel, otherwise the sound of fist-banging or finger-drumming will be disastrously magnified. Also be sure the microphone is facing your narrator. You can compensate for the direction of the microphone by being aware that you, the interviewer, should speak louder.

If the floor is covered with a rug, don't place the tape recorder directly on it, especially if your machine is ventilated from the bottom. Fibers from the rug can be sucked into the machine and interfere with or ruin the recording.

53

While you are setting up your equipment, you will want to chat informally with your interviewee about the weather, his health—anything in order to make the narrator feel at ease. Don't take too long or the interviewee will begin to feel nervous. Sit down near the interviewee at conversation distance. The farther away you are from the narrator, the more difficult it will be to establish rapport. At least four feet away is a good distance; ten feet is too far.

There are about five seconds of tape which cannot record, so allow a lead-in of ten seconds plus a little extra. Record a formal introduction to the tape before the interview. The formal introduction should sound something like this:

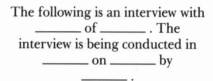

The following is an interview with
_____ of _____ . The
interview is being conducted in
_____ on _____ by
_____ .

Tape your introduction in your home before you do the interview. Should you make a mistake or not be satisfied with the outcome, simply rewind the tape and begin again. Then leave the machine exactly where you completed your introduction. This is where the interview will begin. Do not play the introduction for your interviewee as it may sound formal and intimidating to him.

Conducting the Interview

When you are both seated, with the microphone in place and turned on, you can casually ease your way into the interview. You may chat informally while you are setting up your equipment. But you should tell your subject when you are beginning the actual interview. Then press down the *play* and *record* buttons, and if you have an external microphone make sure it is in the *on* position. After a few moments, you can hold up your finger to indicate a pause to check that the recording is going well. Rewind the tape. Make sure you can hear the tape properly. Unless you check on your machine, you run the risk of arriving home and discovering that your interview was a total loss. Once an interviewer completed her interview, went home, played her tape back, and found it to be running very slowly. Checking her machine, she saw that the batteries had been left in. She had recorded on run-down batteries instead of using the wall outlet—because the electrical plug was improperly attached. Never record with batteries in the machine unless there is no wall outlet at all—on an airplane or bus, for instance. Ideally, do not store your batteries in your machine. Should the batteries leak, they will ruin the tape recorder.

The first few minutes of recording are crucial in setting the tone of the interview. You want the interview to be informal, relaxed, and calm. Therefore, do not begin the session by asking a controversial question or baiting the interviewee. You have supposedly chosen a relative whom you admire, respect, and think you can record for the best family history. Don't antagonize him. Save the more delicate questions until you and the narrator have established a good rapport. If you can ask an open-ended question after the first few closed ones requiring name, date, and place of birth, so much the better. Giving the interviewee a chance to spin out his tale will help him to forget that all his words are being taken up by the microphone. While apprehensive at first about recording, most people love to talk about themselves and quickly get into the spirit of the interview. For many, it can become a therapeutic experience.

Most important of all, your role is to fade away as much as possible. You are the catalyst—you provide the brief questions— but then get out of the way. During the interview, try not to make confirming sounds like "uh-huh" or "yup," but rather to nod your head while a story is being told. "Uh-huhs" are very annoying to listen to when a tape is replayed.

Also, remember to ask one question at a time. Look directly at the narrator when you ask your question. Don't fiddle with the machine while asking questions as it reminds the narrator that he isn't just conversing with you, and can lead to "mike-fright." Naturally, your one question can lead to other questions, but you don't want to be so eager to ask the other questions that you interrupt your relative. Remember, it's his interview, not yours.

Write down on your pad the questions that do occur to you while your narrator is speaking. You can either ask them when a particular anecdote is completed or after the session is concluded. Sometimes the narrator can lose track of what he was saying and it's your job to remind him of where he was. So be alert.

On one tape of a relative, the narrator began speaking about her grandmother and then branched off to her grandfather.

> I loved my grandmother. She was a sweet . . . She was taller than my grandfather. My grandfather looked like you would say a fellow of the Confederate Army. He wore a broad-brimmed hat—in the middle, you know, he'd have that dent. He was a sweet old man and he was very fond of my mother. He—I don't remember what I was talking about.

The interviewer had been listening carefully and was able to guide the narrator back to her original anecdote by reminding her that "You were telling me about your grandmother." The narrator continued with a very valuable reminiscence about her grandmother's cooking.

Sometimes a narrator will pause long before going on to his next sentence or story. Don't feel that you must jump in with another question. A period of silence is often just a way for the narrator to gather up his thoughts or pause for breath before continuing. If you rush in with a question that may or may not be related to what the narrator was going to say, he may forget the important anecdote he wanted to tell you. While he pauses, you can write down a note or two on your pad—or pretend to write something down. Don't be afraid to let the tape run. It's not like a television show where silence is the ultimate sin.

When you listen to an interview on television or radio, the questions the interviewer asks seem so perfectly phrased. You may feel that your questions are awkward in comparison. Remember that television interviewers are professionals following a script prepared by others. You, on the other hand, did the background research and handled all steps in the interview process yourself. You know your material, but you do not have to appear as an expert. The person you are interviewing probably isn't an expert either. Your mistakes will put him at ease and make him more comfortable. False starts on questions are a very frequent part of unedited tapes. If you don't like the way it sounds, you can transcribe the tape and write it up into an edited text.

One problem that you might have when you are interviewing a relative is getting him to describe other family members. Sometimes you can ease the relative into excellent personality descriptions by having him talk about physical characteristics first. In this excerpt from a tape, the narrator was asked, "Why don't you tell me more about some of your . . . brothers and sisters?" The narrator replied first with physical descriptions, but as she warmed up to her subject and remembered more, she spoke about her siblings' personalities:

> We all looked different. There isn't a resemblance between any one of us in the family. You'd never know we were brothers and sisters. . . .
>
> Then my older brother was a difficult person. We kids really didn't get along with him. Then Rick and I were very close, my brother, Richard, were very close friends. Then I came. I was the next one in the family, and Walter was younger. Walter had an entirely different set of friends. I didn't know too much about them. But Walter was a real good kid and [Rick] and I used to take advantage of him. We'd buy chocolate almonds, eighteen for a nickel, and then we'd divide them [and eat them]. Walter would hold on to them, and then we'd get his, too.

Be sure to use the pencil and paper you have brought with you for note-taking. During the interview there will be names of places and people which you might not be able to spell. Jot them down as phonetically as you can and then go over them with the narrator after the recording machine is turned off.

Another reason to take notes is to pull the narrator back on the track of his family history if he should stray far from the subject. Don't interrupt a good story when the interviewee is in the middle of an anedcote, but do put down a follow-up question to help return to the original path.

Of course, while you are conducting the interview you will be watching the recording machine to make sure the tape doesn't run out. Be sure to bring a large watch with you that you can glance at casually, with ease, without fumbling around to see what time it is. Remember how long each side of your tape runs. Whenever you must break to change the cassette, slide back into the topic you were discussing so that continuity will be kept, e.g., ". . . You were telling me about when your grandmother was taken away by the Indians."

Try to avoid turning the microphone or the recorder on and off. We have found that if you must turn off the machine, it is best to use the controls on the machine itself. The machine will stop immediately, but if you use the mike switch, you will create a slag on the tape. After you have done your five-minute check, there should be no other stops or starts, if possible, except to turn over or to change cassettes. If for some reason, something isn't working properly, apologize profusely, check on the machine, and begin again.

Sometimes the narrator will ask you to turn off the machine because he doesn't want to record a particular story saying it is only background. This may lead to a series of "off-the-record" anecdotes, stops and starts on the tape, and an unconnected interview with the best stories unavailable to your grandchildren. Tell the narrator that you would prefer to record everything now and that he can relate that particular story when the interview is over. Quite often, the interviewee will proceed with his story at this point. If not, it is better to preserve a good relationship with the narrator than to antagonize him by badgering him to tell a story he would rather drop.

There are many ways of narrating a story. If you are interviewing a relative about an event of historical importance or taping a person talking about his business experiences, there may be clashes of fact between the narrator's story and the one you may have heard before. Do not barge in tactlessly and say "That isn't true." Suggest that you have heard a different version of the story, tell it to him, and then ask the narrator to elaborate on his story. Or ask a series of closed questions that deal with facts rather than anecdotes. You may not be able to discover the "truth," but you certainly will see another side of the story.

We have found that very few people purposely tell falsehoods on tape. Sometimes they have perfected a certain way of telling a story that they know will elicit a favorable response from an audience, such as amazement, laughter, or outrage. The perfected story may not be factually true, but it is exciting. This is fine for family anecdotes. However, in searching for historical or business facts, you might prefer to ask a number of questions around the story to see if the later facts square with the earlier story. This is a touchy, yet often important area, so be sure not to appear suspicious of the interviewee's truthfulness or you may have difficulty continuing the interview in a pleasant atmosphere.

Ask the narrator if he participated directly in the event or whether he just heard about it. If he was a participant, you may receive a new historical insight into the occurrence. A woman who had worked in the Triangle Shirtwaist Factory revealed that although fireproofing and compliance with other inspection laws were required after the infamous Triangle Fire of 1916, nevertheless the factory owners continued to break the law. She said,

> Otherwise, they (the factory owners) continued to do it the same way. If a girl wasn't sixteen and the inspector came (to check on the ages of laborers), the owner told her to go to the bathroom—so he wouldn't be fined.

The interviewer then questioned whether the inspectors knew about the violations of the law.

> Yes. Of course it was graft. The same as today. Nothing was said.

Finally, watch your interviewee for signs of fatigue. Sometimes an older person will tire after one hour of interviewing. On the

59

other hand, some narrators are willing to talk on beyond your normal span of concentration. Try to continue as long as the interviewee seems to be proceeding happily. We have found that a three to six hour session on a Sunday—when the interviewee is away from the office or other daily chores and errands—is the best time to interview. Try to interview your average, healthy person in one session. We have discovered that in most instances, subsequent sessions yield little new information and frequently give the interviewee a chance to repeat those stories already told in the first session.

When you end the interview, do it gracefully. Be sure to thank the interviewee for his time. And be sure to go over your notes with him or her to correct names, dates, and spellings. Set up a time and date for the next interview, if necessary, or tell him when you will send a copy of the tapes. Have him or her sign release forms (chapter 10).

Pack up your cassettes, machine, and other equipment carefully. Place each cassette back in the original hard plastic container and label the tape in the blank spaces provided for the name of the narrator, the sequence of the tape, the date, and your name. Also, if the tape is completed, punch in the tabs on the top edge of the tape in order to avoid accidental re-recording of the tape. You now have with you a person's encapsulated life—treat it with respect.

7

Indexing and Making
a Glossary

After you have finished the oral history interview, you have the history, stories and anecdotes you were seeking. And you can listen to them whenever you choose. To complete the job, do the following two steps:

- Record the formal conclusion using this format:
This concludes the interview with _____. The interviewer was _____. The interview took place on _____ in _____.
- Make a duplicate tape for safekeeping.
- Place all cassettes in their labeled plastic containers.

To make the oral history even more accessible and meaningful, you can index and transcribe the tapes.

Indexing

Like a table of contents at the beginning of a book, an index to a tape informs the listener about where to find specific information. Clearly, it is one of the best ways to organize history and to make it available to your future audience. A useful index describes major events, anecdotes, and stories. Your completed index will convey the biography of an individual or the history of a community, just as a well-written book would. It should include all relevant material but omit names or events just mentioned in passing but unimportant in the interview. One would not index "Millard Fillmore" if the narrator says, "Franklin Pierce succeeded Millard Fillmore as president of the United States."

To prepare the index may appear somewhat overwhelming, for it may require hours of hard work sifting through the already taped interview to develop an outline and to highlight important subjects. While listening to the tape, think about organizing the material into related sections. If you have recorded the interview yourself, you will know the general format. Try to create the index as soon as possible after the interview since a fresh memory makes the task much easier. If you did not conduct the interview, you should listen to all the tapes carefully to understand the interviewer's purpose. Then begin working on the index.

Always keep in mind the purpose of the completed index. Is it for family use or research purposes?

If you are preparing an index for your own family, you may want it to be quite specific and detailed. References to important family anecdotes, songs, and stories should be written clearly in the index. However, if the tape is being produced for a business or community organization, the index may take on a different emphasis. Not every anecdote or detailed story need be listed. The index for public usage should reflect what other researchers might be interested in.

In order to define and describe the exact placement of events within the tape, you need a guide to the tape. Since the tape runs for a certain number of minutes per side, one of the ways to pinpoint stories is to state where the story occurs in relation to the time that has elapsed from the beginning of the tape. This is called a "time-segment" index.

Although some tape recorders have a digital counter that marks how many revolutions the supply reel makes, we don't recommend it for indexing work. The reason is that digital counters can vary from machine to machine and thus are not accurate if you use the tape in any recorder other than your own. Also, over a period of time the tape expands and contracts with use, so that the story segment will be at a different place on the counter after many replays. Instead of the digital counter, we suggest you use a large stop watch with minute and second counter to mark off your tape.

A time-segment outline should look something like this:

Lenoir Hood Miller

Time Segment   Volume I, Side 1

0–11 minutes   I. Family Origins
                                    A. Ethel Lenoir Hood born on September 30, 1888, in Glidden, Iowa, the last of nine children, to John Andrew Hood (born 1842) and Amanda Melvina Sears (born 1846).
                                    B. Maternal Grandparents: Did not know well; from Indiana; the big pocket in Grandma Sears' skirt.
                                    C. Paternal Grandparents: Nancy Caroline Tuttle marries John Andrew Washington Hood; John Andrew was one of thirteen children; grew up in Lenoir, North Carolina; at age 10, in 1852, the family sold their slaves and moved to Greencastle, Indiana; the plantation in Lenoir; anecdote about Nancy Caroline selling her slaves.

Time Segment	Volume I, Side 1
11–17 minutes	D. Father:
	John Andrew Hood; member of the 51st Indiana Volunteers for the Civil War; experiences in prison; the prisoner exchange; surgery on the battlefield; the note in the barrel of sawdust; the escape out of prison; the horse and buggy as a trade-in for some land; Decoration Day parades; his physical appearance; anecdote about Daddy Hood and Bobby.
17–26 minutes	E. Mother:
	Amanda Melvina Sears; how she met John Andrew Hood; Amanda's feelings about college; Netty and her musical skills; Guerne at dental school; the other children; the Dean's poem "On Being 80"; Amanda's poor health.

End of Volume I, Side 1

This time-segment index of Lenoir Hood Miller took twenty-six minutes to listen to and about an equal amount of time to organize. Don't forget that typing takes time, too.

You may indicate the organization of the two sides of tape in any fashion you choose, but we have found it useful to refer to each completed cassette as a *volume*. We divide each *volume* into two *sides*, each side consuming one-half of the tape. When the index for the second side of tape begins, our heading reads: Volume I, Side 2—and begins again at "0" minutes.

Sometimes it is hard to see the inherent structure in the taped interview. Therefore, it may be difficult to organize the written index in outline form. You may prefer to write a brief running commentary to index the taped interview. Below is an example of this form:

Lenoir Hood Miller

Volume I, Side I

Ethel Lenoir Hood born September 30, 1888, in Glidden, Iowa, last of nine children, to John Andrew Hood (born 1842) and Amanda Melvina Sears (born 1846). Did not know maternal grandparents well; from Indiana; the big pocket in Grandma Sears' skirt. Paternal grandparents: Nancy Caroline Tuttle marries John Andrew Washington Hood, one of thirteen children; grew up in Lenoir, North Carolina; at age 10, in 1852, family sold their slaves and moved to Greencastle, Indiana; plantation in Lenoir; anecdote about Nancy Caroline selling her slaves. Father: John Andrew Hood; member of the 51st Indiana Volunteers for the Civil War; experiences in prison; prisoner exchange; surgery on the battlefield; the note in the barrel of sawdust; escape out of prison; the horse and buggy as a trade-in for some land; Decoration Day parades; his physical appearance; anecdote about Daddy Hood and Bobby. Mother: Amanda Melvina Sears; how she met John Andrew Hood; Amanda's feelings about college; Netty and her musical skills; Guerne at dental school; the other children; the Dean's poem "On Being 80"; Amanda's poor health.

End of Volume I, Side I

The Glossary

To write a glossary—or explanation—of terms, mark down any unusual words while listening to the tape. Some foreign words may not even sound unusual to you, since you may have heard them so often. Therefore, it is important to be particularly discriminating and to listen carefully to the tape. Old-fashioned words and phrases give individual flavor to your tapes, but they may be meaningless to future generations unless you provide an adequate explanation of them.

The glossary should be written alphabetically, of course, but you should also include a guide for pronunciation as well as an explanation of the words.

Sample Glossary:

BET HAMIDRASH	A house of study.
BEMA	The altar in a synagogue.
BOBE	A grandmother.
CHAZZEN	A cantor, i.e., a professional singer who assists the rabbi.
CHOLENT	A casserole of beans and vegetables usually served on the Sabbath.
DAVEN	To pray.
DRUSE	A member of a sect in Syria, Lebanon, and Israel whose primarily Moslem religion contains some elements of Christianity. In Israel, they are sympathetic to the Jewish State, and at their own request serve in the Israeli Army.

When you have completed the index and glossary (if necessary), you will possess an excellent guide to the recorded tapes. Anyone who wishes to listen to the tapes will be well informed of what to expect. The index and glossary give added meaning to the tape while allowing it to be used to capture the nuances of the narrator's voice and the many details of his or her life history.

8

Transcribing the Tapes

Transcribing

To preserve the oral history in written form, you can transcribe the complete interview from the tape. This verbatim record consumes time, effort and money. While it is an optional process, it is extremely worthwhile. When you wish to read a relative's words rather than to hear them spoken; when you don't have the time to listen through a lengthy section of tape; and when you want to retrieve just one special family story, then having the written account is a tremendous time-saver. A transcript is a helpful companion to a recorded tape. Sometimes, too, the unexpected can happen—accidental erasures because of failure to punch the tape tabs or exposure to magnetic fields, and at least there will be a written record. Also, if you decide to send some of the material to other relatives or to use the information in magazine or newspaper articles, a written transcript is an absolute necessity.

You may transcribe the tapes yourself or hire someone to do the job. Working with a word processor makes it easier to type from the tape and correct when necessary. In addition, you can store the written record on a disk as well as on the printed page. Transcribing from tape does take time—anywhere from six to twenty hours of typing and editing per hour of tape—depending on the clarity of the tape, accents, and the skill of the transcriber. It is possible to transcribe directly from the tape, do minor editing, and type a rough copy of the interview. We recommend doing this only if you are a moderately accomplished typist. A foot pedal can be attached to most machines. This helps the transcribing process by allowing you to start and to stop the tape without removing your hands from the keyboard. On the other hand, you may get the same slag with the foot pedal as you do when using the microphone *on-off* switch. Since the tape may slur words and advance faster than your typing, you may need to operate the machine manually to hear all parts of the tape.

If you are transcribing in a busy room, it is handy to use a headphone set which attaches to any tape recorder. Most machines come with an earphone, which we find too flimsy to place securely in your ear while you are typing. A headphone set is far more stable. Headsets allow you to concentrate on the tape and not disturb or be disturbed by others in the room. If you are planning to transcribe in a quiet place, you may not need the headset or earphone, but you may decide to use the foot pedal.

If you have access to a dictating machine which takes a full-size cassette, this would have a foot pedal, headset and reverse mechanisms already attached. Otherwise, use the regular tape recorder with foot pedal and/or headphone. Of course, you can always write out the transcript in long-hand and then type it yourself or have someone else do that for you. Typing charges vary and could cost approximately $3.50/page or $12–$25/hour.

To transcribe requires concentration and quiet. Because of the rise and fall in intonation during taping, it may be difficult to hear some parts of the conversation on tape. That is why it's best to transcribe the tape as soon as possible. You will be more familiar with what the narrator said and thus better able to decipher garbled phrases. Even so, you may not be able to catch all the words in every sentence. In that case, you may want to telephone the person interviewed and review the tape with him.

You will probably need to do at least two transcriptions from the tape itself. On the first "translation," write down the exact words as spoken, including repetitions of phrases, hesitations, extraneous encouraging words from the interviewer like "Is that so?", and grammatical errors. Leave blank spaces where you cannot hear the words, and put question marks next to phrases or spellings that are unclear. Be prepared to listen over and over again to the same phrase until it sounds right. Make sure that you double-space your manuscript or that you leave enough space to add later corrections. Of course, working with a word processor makes editing text much easier. If you type, you might want to make two copies of the original transcription so that you can write corrections on one and retain the original as a checking copy.

If you have already written an index to your tape, you will know what subjects will be covered by the narrator at approximately what point on the tape. This is a distinct help in understanding the words of the interviewee. Nevertheless, you will probably have a fragmented-looking text on the first transcription unless you have decided to do some minor editing while transcribing.

Composing a Narrative Account

There is a debate between those oral historians who believe a transcript should contain the exact words of the narrator and interviewer, stumbles and all, and those who claim that slight editing is permissible. The purists say that an unedited text gives a more complete, realistic view of how the person actually speaks and thinks. However, it is difficult to follow an unedited text. Slight editing, deleting false starts, clarifying questions, removing speech hesitations like "uhs," make the transcript far more readable. When deciding which approach you want to use, consider your goal—a readable text or a verbatim report of family history.

This is an example of how one unedited interviewing session sounded on tape, certainly not perfect. It is followed by the edited written text.

Original Tape

Question: Let me just ask you . . . which . . . you . . . all these people . . . Do you remember your Grandparents Lee?

Answer: I remember . . . I don't remember my grandfather. I remember my mother's brother, Uncle John Lee. But Uncle John Lee and uh . . . and one of the Lee's sisters and mother . . . three of them, I'm sure the children . . . and uh . . . mother and John were captured by the Indians. And the parents were all killed. But those three children . . . John Lee, I remember him. While I went out . . . When I went out to California, near the desert. When I went out there, John Lee was still living. He's passed away now, but he was still living. He's passed away now, but he was still living.

Question: Wait a minute, your Grandmother Lee was killed by the Indians?

Answer: My grand . . . My mother's mother's father and some of her sisters and brothers were all killed by the Indians.

Generally, oral historians are taking a middle view—leaving in grammatical errors if they form part of the narrator's natural speech pattern; removing inconsistencies if the narrator had an obvious slip of the tongue. Certain guidelines emerge:

- Do not remove regional expressions.
- Remove false starts in questions or answers.
- Omit encouraging comments such as "uh-huh," "I see," "yes?" which destroy the narrative's continuity.
- Indicate obvious non-verbal actions in brackets, for example, laughter, crying, pounding on table.

Edited Text

Question: Do you remember your Grandparents Lee?

Answer: I don't remember my grandfather. I remember my mother's brother, Uncle John Lee. But Uncle John Lee and one of the Lee sisters and mother—three of them, I'm sure—the children, mother, and John—were captured by the Indians. And the parents were all killed.

John Lee, I remember him. When I went out to California, near the desert, John Lee was still living. He's passed away now, but he was still living.

70

Question: Your Grandmother Lee was killed by the Indians?
Answer: My mother's mother's father and some of her sisters
 and brothers were all killed by the Indians.

You may decide later to significantly edit your transcript, but you should keep the original text around for its value in comparison. Also, if you are taping a famous relative and plan to use some portion of the transcription in published form, be sure to check with your narrator on your edited portions of the tape. You must have his or her approval for the use of edited tapes (see chapter 10 on legal forms). Family lawsuits are not unknown. Besides using care in transcribing verbatim and editing, you will want to exercise caution in punctuation and spelling. Correct spelling can be the key to certain family stories, as in this example:

And then my father's English, while it was understandable, was not perfect. He had to write checks and things. And I remember writing out for him a list of how you spell "ten," "twenty," "thirty," "forty"; "one," "two," "three," etc. And he had particular difficulty with forty. He didn't understand why you didn't spell it "fourty" instead of "forty." So I had a list which he pasted up, and when he wrote checks he just followed from my list.

Often judgment in punctuating is up to you. Should you use a dash, three dots, a period? It depends on the context of the sentence. A dash can be used to indicate further explanation of the subject at hand; three dots to indicate a hesitation in speech or a change of subject; and, of course, a period to end a sentence even if the original tape narration does not indicate a stoppage in the interviewee's speech pattern.

On the title page of your final transcript, you might want to use this format:

Oral History Interview
with
Name of Participant
Date
Location
By (Interviewer)

71

The first page would then begin the actual interview. In order to indicate who is speaking, write out your entire name before the first question you ask. After your name place a colon, leave two spaces, and type out the question. Questions should be double-spaced; responses single-spaced. Use the complete name of the interviewee on the first response, followed also by a colon, two spaces, and the reply. Then use "Q" and "A" only, followed by the same punctuation as above. For easy reading, you might want to "box" questions and answers in the format followed by the examples in this book:

Volume I, Side I

Ellen Robinson Epstein: Tell me your complete name.
Martha Lehman: My name? My maiden name or my marriage name? My name was Martha Rachel Lewit. Then I married Milton Lewis, and when he died, I was a widow for a couple of years and then I married a person by the name of Mark Lehman. All M. L.'s
ERE: Where and when were you born?
ML: I was born October 3, 1899, in Newark.

In order to retain as much of the flavor of the original tape as possible, do put in editorial comments in brackets—but don't overdo it. If the narrator emphasizes a point by pounding his fist on a chair, write (pounds fist on chair). If the interviewee cries or laughs in remembering a story, write (cries) or (laughs). In this example, the narrator's laughter was an important part of her story:

There was one friend of mine at college. She wasn't a close friend. She was a gal who was in one of my classes and we were going home for Christmas. I happened to sit with her on the train and the train was very late—snow storm and what not—and was held up. She said "Why don't you come home and have lunch with me?" So—okay. So I did.
The way she dressed, my goodness, well, some old shirt or something about the way people go around nowadays. My

mother wouldn't have wanted me to wear anything that looked like that. But she was met by a chauffeur and a big car, and [we were] taken to this house.

The door was opened by a butler. I'd never seen one before and I about dropped dead, and the rugs, you know, you just sunk into the rugs like this [pushes feet on the floor]. She had a charming mother and aunt, I guess, and they were just as sweet as they could be, but I was so tongue-tied that it was a while that I could hardly say anything. They suggested that I might want to phone my mother that I was to be so late, but we didn't have any phone [laughter] so I had to call a neighbor's. Then there was the silver, and a bare table with beautiful linen doilies on it which I wasn't used to. Then I had to watch which spoon to use for the dessert 'cause I thought I was taking it all in but I'm afraid I wasn't much of a guest [more laughter].

Be sure to transcribe the questions as well as the replies. Sometimes, in the interest of obtaining a continuous story, transcribers leave out the interviewer's questions. This gives a false and often inconsistent picture of the narrator. It is far more interesting to have both the interviewer's questions and the interviewee's answers included in the transcript. There is such a thing as overzealous editing. The following example show a severely pruned transcription without including the questions from the interviewer, and then the same tape, including questions, with very slight editing.

Edited Transcription Without Questions

Well, I think I was always a suffragette. I was active in that organization and I had a friend, and we also went to the Educational Alliance. Then a friend heard about this—the movement that women would get the vote—and, of course, I was always interested in reading the newspapers and things, and I read about this and my oldest brother was also interested. We'd be discussing these things, and I thought it was very good things, and he said, "Oh, you gonna be a fool. What do you want to be doing that and doing those things?" But my mother said "Oh, that's wonderful."

73

We went to different people's homes, and (what was that woman's name?) a very popular, prominent woman that we had a meeting in her house. She lived on Fifth Avenue and my friends and I, we went to this woman's house. And off the mantlepiece she served tea and cookies. Moved all the furniture out of the room and we were introduced to this movement, the suffragette movement.

I went to the meetings which were held in Clinton Hall, which was a very popular place for Socialist people. It was a building where people came together and had meetings.

Different societies had club rooms there. And we met there. About once a week, we'd go. The Henry Street Settlement also had that. Just women came, maybe fifty.

Of course, I marched in a parade on a Saturday and I walked all the way from Lewis Street, where we lived on the East Side, to this big rally. And my mother went with me 'cause she wanted to see me march.

Whitelaw Reid. Mrs. Whitelaw Reid—she led it in a white outfit that she wore every year that we had the parade.

Edited Transcription with Questions from Interviewer

Answer: Well, I think I was always a suffragette, and I was active in that organization.

Question: How did you become interested in that?

Answer: I had a friend and we also went to the Educational Alliance and then a friend heard about this, the movement that women would get the vote and, of course, I was always interested in reading the newspapers and things, and I read about this. And my oldest brother was also interested, and we'd be discussing these things, and I thought it was very good things, and he said, "Oh, you gonna be a fool. What do you want to be doing that and doing those things?" But my mother said, "Oh, that's wonderful."

And we went to different people's homes and (what was that woman's name?) a very popular, prominent woman that we had a meeting in her house. And she

74

lived on Fifth Avenue, and my friends and I, we went to this woman's house. And off the mantlepiece she served tea and cookies. Moved all the furniture out of the room, and we were introduced to this movement, the suffragette movement.

I went to the meetings which were held in Clinton Hall, which was a very popular place for Socialist people.

Question: What was Clinton Hall?

Answer: It was a building where people came together and had meetings. Different societies had club rooms there. And we met there.

Question: How often did you have the meetings?

Answer: About once a week, we'd go. The Henry Street Settlement also had that.

Question: How many people would attend meetings?

Answer: Oh, well, just the women came. Maybe fifty.

Question: Did you ever march in a parade?

Answer: Of course. I marched in a parade on a Saturday, and I walked all the way from Lewis Street where we lived on the East Side to this big rally. And my mother went with me 'cause she wanted to see me march.

Question: What was the march like? Did you carry placards?

Answer: Whitelaw Reid. Mrs. Whitelaw Reid—she led it in a white outfit that she wore every year that we had the parade.

There are, however, some things you may want to delete and whose deletion will definitely add to the readability of the text. Comments from the interviewer which are clearly meant to encourage the narrator to continue can easily be left out of the transcript. There is no need to write down disconnected phrases like "my gosh" or "for heaven's sake" if they add nothing to the family history. In fact, they will distract attention from the narrator even though in their original context the phrases helped the speaker continue his story. Here is an example of a portion of tape including encouraging "remarks" and the same tape without the intrusive phrases.

Text Containing Interviewer's Extraneous Comments

Question: Were most people completely unaware that a union existed, or did you have to enlighten them that they could have a better life if they joined the union?

Answer: People were afraid to begin with. They were frightened. They were immigrants. Most people were not as well—I wouldn't call myself an educated person but compared to them I was a college graduate. They didn't even know how to read and write.

Question: Really! Is that so?

Answer: They were ignorant people. They were not even concerned with economic situations. I already came from a home where things were happening. My father was a socialist leader. He was a leader who made people conscious of discrimination.

Question: That's very interesting.

Answer: I became a Socialist from reading Tolstoy and Gorky. I was reading literature and my ideas were already enlightened by this exploitation. I tried to help since there was a union and it was the union's business to organize. So they made use of people like me.

Question: Uh huh. Ah, were your parents aware of your activities?

Answer: Yes. They were. My father used to close one eye and my mother was afraid I'd get into trouble. I was arrested several times.

Question: Wow!

Answer: I was in jail about four times. One time I remember we organized a shop down on the East Side on Houston Street, a real sweat shop. It had unsanitary conditions and they underpaid the workers. I worked for them about two weeks and you know, they sensed I was planted there.

Question: This is exciting. What happened next?

Answer: When I felt it was time, we said we were representing the union and asked to conduct a meeting there. Of

76

course, the bosses got very excited and started throwing machines at us and then they called the police.

Question: My goodness!

Answer: The police came and got ahold of me like this. [Grabs her own arm.] And in those days we wore hats. Everybody wore a hat and a hat pin. And I stuck him with my hat pin.

Question: And that's why you were arrested?

Answer: That's why I was arrested. And I was put in jail for a day.

Question: You're kidding!

Answer: And the union employed a lawyer at that time. . . . He was a union lawyer, a very good one. He came to bail me out and get me out of jail. And then the union sent me flowers! But the girls I was in the jail with, they were all prostitutes. And they came over to me and said "What street did you work on?"

Edited Text Without Interviewer's Extraneous Comments

Question: Were most people completely unaware that a union existed, or did you have to enlighten them that they could have a better life if they joined the union?

Answer: People were afraid to begin with. They were immigrants. Most people were not as well—I wouldn't call myself an educated person, but compared to them I was a college graduate. They didn't even know how to read and write. They were ignorant people. They were not even concerned with economic situations. I already came from a home where things were happening. My father was a socialist leader. He was a leader who made people conscious of discrimination.

I became a Socialist from reading Tolstoy and Gorky. I was reading literature and my ideas were already enlightened by this exploitation. I tried to help since there was a union and it made use of people like me.

Question: Were your parents aware of your activities?

77

Answer: Yes. They were. My father used to close one eye and my mother was afraid I'd get into trouble. I was arrested several times. I was in jail about four times. One time I remember we organized a shop down on the East Side on Houston Street, a real sweat shop. It had unsanitary conditions and they underpaid the workers. I worked for them about two weeks and you know, they sensed I was planted there. When I felt it was time, we said we were representing the union and asked to conduct a meeting there. Of course, the bosses got very excited and started throwing machines at us and then they called the police.

The police came and got ahold of me like this. [Grabs her own arm.] And in those days we wore hats. Everybody wore a hat and a hat pin. And I stuck him with my hat pin.

Question: And that's why you were arrested?

Answer: That's why I was arrested. And I was put in jail for a day. And the union employed a lawyer at that time. He was a union lawyer, a very good one. He came to bail me out and get me out of jail. And then the union sent me flowers! But the girls I was in the jail with, they were all prostitutes. And they came over to me and said "What street did you work on?"

Remember to delete extraneous phrases or repeated statements. Write down each sentence accurately to add clarity to your transcript.

Completing the Transcript

There may be a question about whether to submit your unedited manuscript to your relative in order to let him or her see what was said during the interview. Perhaps you will have planned in advance to give only a corrected, final transcript to your interviewee. This is probably the best thing to do, especially if you are using the interview only for a family history. Relatives of the interviewee usually do not cause problems. However, if you give an unedited manuscript to a relative, this may lead to complications. It is often irresistible for a relative to try to revise the text into the way he thinks he should sound rather than the way he actually did sound. Or a relative can change his mind completely about letting you use the tapes for your grandchildren—or for any other purpose—despite legal agreements.

If your oral history is for family use only, and the narrator is adamant about not releasing certain information, you will have to apply your best judgment about how to proceed. If the legal release and agreement is already signed, that should take care of all contingencies (See Chapter 10, Legal Forms). But if you decide to change the wording of these forms, or if your narrator insists on a change, you may or may not be able to use questionable material.

The interviewee, especially if well-known, can be allowed to edit the written manuscript and be given the option of *closing*—not allowing specific portions of or an entire interview to be played for a specified number of years. However, this option means you must have a place to store the tape safely for a period of ten years or perhaps more. For the tapes of a famous individual, it might be best to check with your library or historical society to see if they have such storage facilities. Also, in a community-wide project of historical value, you must consider issues of editing, closing and storing.

Creating a Table of Contents

After the tape has been typed up in manuscript form, the transcript can be used to produce a page number index, exactly like a table of contents. This will be a guide to the transcript, not to the tape itself. Using the page number index system, Lenoir Hood Miller's index would look like this:

Table of Contents

Family Origins	Page Number
A. Date and place of birth of Lenoir Hood Miller. Parents' names and dates of birth.	1

Family Origins   Page Number

B. Names of maternal   2–3
grandparents. Their ori-
gins. Anecdote about
Grandma Sears' skirt
pocket.

C. Paternal grandparents.   4–6
The slave plantation in
Greencastle, Indiana.
The plantation in Lenoir.
Nancy Caroline sells her
slaves.

D. Father: John Andrew   6–10
Hood. His Civil War ex-
periences. He trades his
horse and buggy for
some land. Decoration
Day parades. His physical
appearance. Story about
Daddy Hood and Bobby.

E. Mother: Amanda Melvina   10–15
Sears. Her marriage. Her
feelings about college.
Anecdotes: Netty and her
musical skills; Guerne at
dental school. The other
children. Old age: the
Dean's poem; poor
health.

Adding Photographs and Other Memorabilia

Now is the time to select from your collection of old family photographs. Adding visual memories to your transcript will greatly enhance your finished product. If you are making a very limited number of books, you can duplicate the photos and mount each individually in the book. If you no longer have the negative, you can inexpensively make a copy-negative and then reproduce the number of photos you need. These can neatly go into your book if you use random mount plastic photo sleeves, which have sticky backs and adhere anywhere.

If you are making a larger number of books, you have two options:

• Go to the printer with all your photos and ask him to make a half-tone for each. The printer will be able to copy a black and white photo so that it looks like a photo in a book. After making one half-tone from your original, he can then photocopy as many as you need for your books.

• Find a printer who has a Xerox machine specially made to copy black and white photographs. By adjusting the light and dark controls on the duplicating machine, one can copy originals quite nicely.

Whichever technique you choose for duplicating your pictures, be sure that you identify each photo with a typed caption that includes names, date and location. Perhaps you might also like to add ticket stubs, maps, and old letters. This is the time to dig through your attic boxes for memories of the past. These items will add an old-fashioned scrapbook quality to your oral history project.

Binding the Final Copy

When you have completely edited and typed a final copy of the transcript, you might want to bind the manuscript into book form. This will preserve the transcript and make it easier to read. You can go to an *instant* printer such as Copy King, Kinko, Minuteman, Quick Copy, or whoever is in your neighborhood. The printer can help you select a plastic spiral or paperback binding for the finished product. A hardback binding is more difficult to find. One inexpensive method we have used is Velo-Bind, which is a long-lasting way to bind books. There may be other options in your price range. We recommend that you call a number of printers to see what your choices are. All this effort will lead to well preserved memories that can be shared proudly.

William and Elizabeth Ragnowitz Lewit
c. 1881.

The twins Arthur and Herbert Levine
New York City, c. 1912.

82

Pauline Resnick and Benjamin Wolman
Holyoke, Massachusetts, January 1903
just prior to their marriage on April 7, 1903.

The marriage of Jessica Wolman and Arthur Levine
New York City, March 6, 1935.

Jessica and Arthur Levine on their second wedding anniversary
Atlantic City, March 6, 1937.

Martha and Walter Lewit on their family's front porch.
Newark, New Jersey, c. 1907.

9

Oral History for Classroom Use

For most of human history, professional historians have focused on the actions and decisions of the elite—pharoahs, kings, emperors, popes—in shaping events. Meanwhile, the common people conducted their unheralded daily lives, making their own form of history. Today, many revisionist historians and others believe that the individual and cumulative acts of ordinary citizens merit study. In the past, the history of the common person was preserved through oral tradition or storytelling, often overlaid with ritual. Today, students can use the tape recorder to preserve the history of everyday people.

In high school or college classes, students can have a hands-on learning experience by participating in a oral history project. While reading textbooks or original documents may give needed background, conducting an oral history interview can bring history to life. In older communities, students have interviewed elderly citizens about the crafts practiced in the past or about how a city looked before urban renewal. In new communities, oral historians have searched for the original owners of now developed land in order to record their memories. Recording an oral history of one's own community enhances a sense of the past and preserves it for the future. Not only do students learn firsthand about their own environment, but they can also pass on the tapes and transcripts to future students and historians.

In gathering an oral history of various aspects of the local community, students may also find they are performing an important service to elderly citizens. The students, in effect, are valuing the interviewee. By spending time with people whose life experiences have often been regarded at best irrelevant, the interviewer proves to the narrator that his memories and his life are, indeed, valuable. Letting older citizens express their feelings, listening to their stories, recording their traditions, are ways of showing the worth of an individual. While the student receives insights into his community, the senior citizen also gains the opportunity of passing on his skills, knowledge, and experience to another generation.

When asked his opinion of an oral history interview, one older interviewee, now living in a nursing home, said:

> You know, I fell into bed that night. I didn't know anymore if I was Mr. X, or a wet rag, but it felt good to put my whole life together.*

The recording of oral history tapes in a community enables students and teachers to learn from the past and to study the values which bind together various groups. By studying the past, students may understand what needs protection for the future—ceremonies, traditions, skills, music, art, architecture. Oral history isn't writing about history; it's listening to history as it was lived.

The nation's first organized oral history program was begun in 1948 by the historian Allan Nevins of Columbia University. His purpose was basically elitist—to record the experiences of well-known American citizens in order to provide fuller insights into historical events. The Columbia collection now has tapes of more than twenty-seven hundred, including about one-half mil-

---

*"Remembering, Reminiscing, and Life," Shulamith Weisman and Rochelle Shusterman, *Concern* magazine, December–January, 1977, p. 23.

lion pages of transcript. The Oral History Research Office at Columbia is involved in obtaining oral history interviews, preserving the tapes, and publicizing their value. A bibliography of their holdings is available from the Oral History Collection, Box 20, Butler Library, Columbia University, New York, New York 10027.

More recently, other historians have researched less famous people and ethnic groups. One of the most important—and most financially and culturally successful—projects is the "Foxfire" program begun in the middle sixties by Eliot Wigginton. This program, originally started as a quarterly magazine put out by high school children living in the small northeast Appalachian town of Rabun Gap, Georgia, has burgeoned into a model for nationwide "Foxfire" history projects. The Foxfire project itself recorded the lifestyle, crafts, and survival techniques of local elderly Georgia residents and thus preserved a unique part of American history. Ultimately, the Foxfire project produced many *Foxfire* books which became best-sellers, several other books by Foxfire students, and has inspired more than one hundred other projects in cultural journalism. Students and teachers can find out more about Foxfire by writing the Foxfire Fund, Inc., P.O. Box 541, Mountain City, GA 30562. Or you can call the Teacher Outreach Education Office at (706) 746-5319 or Administrative Office at (706) 746-5828.

Now there are hundreds of oral history programs throughout the U.S.—some university-sponsored and heavily financed, others just grade school classroom projects on a single theme. One high school project resulted in a book, *The Salt Book*, edited by Pamela Wood, on cultural aspects of New England in the past and present. Other projects are still underway to discover such diverse traditions as social, cultural, and economic integration of Puerto Rican women in New York, 1920–1948; Jewish life in rural America; women in medicine; a videotape of workers who participated in the WPA program for federal theaters; early Greek residents of Oregon; the nursing profession in the state of Arkansas; early aeronautics in Utah; people who survived the big flood in South Dakota; country music and its various facets—

producers, song-writers, businessmen, booking agents, and sing-
ers; the Citadel's (military academy in South Carolina) program
on war and society; an oral history of forty retired Texas ran-
gers; and personal recollections of Greenwich, Connecticut,
citizens who lived from 1890–1970. In other words, oral history
is a project that everyone can become involved in. It can begin
with one's own family and can branch out into the recording of
the lifestyle of an entire community.

To begin an oral history program in a classroom, the teacher
or student leader should write to the Oral History Association,
P.O. Box 3968, Albuquerque, NM 87190-3968, (505) 277-8213,
Attn: Jan Dodson Barnhart, Executive Secretary, to receive a
copy of their Guidelines and possibly to join the organization
itself. The Oral History Association was founded in 1967 and
has thousands of members throughout the world, publishes a
quarterly newsletter, and holds an annual convention. There is
an annual Oral History Review booklet as well. The newsletter
and Review are the best sources for finding out about current
research projects in local communities and current publications
across the country. There are also regional oral history chapters
like the New England Oral History Association, or OHMAR,
Oral History in the Mid-Atlantic Region, which have up-to-date
information on ongoing programs in a specific area. Both the
national and the regional associations are excellent sources for
materials on funding, publications, and people who are also
working in the field. The Association encourages local projects
and membership in their organization.

The Guidelines of the Oral History Association, adopted in
November, 1977, state the ethical responsibilities of both the
interviewer and the interviewee and set forth the obligations of
the amateur historian. The class is free to use materials gathered
according to the agreements entered into with the interviewees.
Understanding the legal agreements and ethical responsibilities
is extremely important in verifying rights to the oral history
interview.

Goals and Guidelines: Oral History Association

Preamble

The Oral History Association recognizes oral history as a method of gathering and preserving historical information in spoken form and encourages those who produce and use oral history to recognize certain principles, rights, and obligations for the creation of source material that is authentic, useful, and reliable.

I. Guidelines for the Interviewee
    A. The interviewee should be informed of the purposes and procedures of oral history in general and of the particular project to which contribution is being made.
    B. In recognition of the importance of oral history to an understanding of the past and in recognition of the costs and effort involved, the interviewee should strive to import candid information of lasting value.
    C. The interviewee should be aware of the mutual rights involved in oral history, such as editing and seal privileges, literary rights, prior use, fiduciary relationships, royalties, and determination of the disposition of all forms of the record and the extent of dissemination and use.
    D. Preferences of the person interviewed and any prior agreements should govern the conduct of the oral history process, and these preferences and agreements should be carefully documented for the record.
II. Guidelines for the Interviewer
    A. Interviewers should guard against possible social injury to or exploitation of interviewees and should conduct interviews with respect for human dignity.
    B. Each interviewee should be selected on the basis of demonstrable potential for imparting information of lasting value.

91

C. The interviewer should strive to prompt informative dialogue through challenging and perceptive inquiry, should be grounded in the background and experiences of the person being interviewed, and, if possible, should review the sources relating to the interviewee before conducting the interview.

D. Interviewers should extend the inquiry beyond their immediate needs to make each interview as complete as possible for the benefit of others and should, whenever possible, place the material in a depository where it will be available for general research.

E. The interviewer should inform the interviewee of the planned conduct of the oral history process and develop mutual expectations of rights connected thereto, including editing, mutual seal privileges, literary rights, prior use, fiduciary relationships, royalties, rights to determine disposition of all forms of the record, and the extent of dissemination and use.

F. Interviews should be conducted in a spirit of objectivity, candor, and integrity, and in keeping with common understandings, purposes, and stipulations mutually arrived at by all parties.

G. The interviewer shall not violate and will protect the seal on any information considered confidential by the interviewee, whether imparted on or off the record.

III. Guidelines for Sponsoring Institutions

A. Subject to conditions prescribed by interviewees, it is an obligation of sponsoring institutions (or individual collectors) to prepare and preserve easily usable records; to keep careful records of the creation and processing of each interview; to identify, index, and catalog interviews; and, when open to research, to make their existence known.

B. Interviewers should be selected on the basis of professional competence and interviewing skill; interviewers should be carefully matched to interviewees.

92

C. Institutions should keep both interviewees and inter-
    viewers aware of the importance of the above Guide-
    lines for the successful production and use of oral
    history sources.

This is a basic document which should be studied carefully in
the classroom before beginning any project.

The oral history interviewer has a double responsibility when
he tapes records for any purpose outside immediate family use.
He is responsible to the narrator and to future historians for the
accuracy and completeness of his recording. In order to fulfill
these responsibilities, the classroom teacher should emphasize
to the class that:

1. The interviewer must clearly tell his interviewee, in writing and
    by phone, what his purpose is in conducting an interview. Why
    the narrator was chosen, what he will be interviewed about, and
    to what use the tapes and/or transcripts will be put should be
    discussed.
2. The interviewer or a legal committee representative should keep
    copies of all correspondence with the narrator. Possible legal
    forms are listed and samples printed in chapter 10 and include
    the pre-recording understanding, the agreement on use, and
    the possible limitation on publication.
3. The interviewer should give the interviewee the opportunity to
    tell his side of the story without interruption of harassment from
    the interviewer. Any conflict with other stories or recordings
    should be handled as delicately as possible, using calm question-
    ing techniques and never stating outright that the interviewee is
    wrong.
4. The class should try to maintain a record of the materials
    recorded so that they can be used by future historians. The
    record should include indexes, and transcripts of all tapes if
    possible, except where limitations on use exist—and these should
    be clearly marked.

Teachers and students may have a specific oral history project
in mind. However, if you are looking for suggestions, topics can

range from the simple to the complex. Below is a list of broad themes which can be studied in various communities:

Land Use	Changes from farming to small industry. Interviews with residents who may have been farmers or worked in factories no longer functioning.
Ethnic Groups	How many are in your town? Who are the leaders? What are the traditions of each group? What is their relationship with other groups?
Architecture	How have buildings changed in your town? Are any of the architects of buildings or homes in your area willing to talk about their work? What were their main purposes in creating their designs? Was there an overall plan?
State or Local Legislators	What programs are politicians particularly involved in? What is the role of party organizations in getting legislators elected? How have parties and issues changed over the years?
A Local Block	What stores were there before? Who worked in them? What was the community like?

Veterans	Which wars were they in? How were the veterans received back after the war? What are their memories of the war?
The Depression	How did your town survive? How did local residents cope? What do they remember about belt-tightening measures?
Local Crafts and Folklore	What techniques are special to your area? How are those crafts practiced? How were people taught crafts? Where were materials gathered? What was done with the finished product?
Resort Communities	What was the area like before the tourists arrived? Who changed jobs to accommodate tourists—why and how? What do the local residents think of the newcomers?
Factory Towns	Who remembers when the factory was built? How did lifestyles change? The effect of unionization, if any? Different jobs within the factory—how are they done and what do people think of their work?

The keys to a good oral history project are organization and careful delegation of work. Once a project has been decided upon by the class, committees should be set up with a leader for each committee. Suggested committees are:

Equipment	This group would be in charge of procuring the necessary tape recorders, cassettes, microphones, notepads, pencils, and transcribing materials. The availability of at least two machines is recommended. The group should also maintain the machines or be able to call upon professionals to give advice.
Interviewee Selection Committee	Researches possible people to interview about the subject to be recorded. Contacts them by phone or writes a preliminary questionnaire, sends the forms and letters to verify the interviews. Chooses the interviewees.
Background Research Committee	Seeks out all possible information about the people finally selected to be interviewed. Briefs interviewers either orally or in writing about the narrators they will record. Prepares outline of questions with interviewers.
Interviewers' Committee	Does the actual interviewing. Must be quiet, calm types able to cope with equipment and many different personalities. Good listeners make the best interviewers. Conducts the oral history interview and completes the tape.
Indexing and Transcribing Committee	Listens to the tapes with the interviewer and writes up a time-

segment index for each tape. The indexer for a tape should also be the transcriber if the group decides to transcribe. A possible variation of this committee is a team consisting of the interviewer, an indexer, and a transcriber. Indexers and transcribers should be able to type and be patient enough to listen to many hours of tape.

Storage and Tape Maintenance Committee

Takes the completed tapes, indexes, and transcripts and keeps them in a special file cabinet or arranges to have them placed in a local library or historical society office for safekeeping. Maintains a record of which people have been recorded, which tapes are available or have been sealed for future use, and listens to tapes once or twice a year to see that they are in good condition. Informs class or public about tape topics. Prepares index cards about tapes which include name of subject, number of tapes, dates interviewed, whether transcribed or not, lists, briefly, contents of tape.

Legal Committee

Provides forms for pre-recording understanding, release forms, limitations on publication, agreements on use. Maintains file of agreements. A copy of the release form should be placed in every transcript as well. Oversees adherence to the Guidelines of the Oral History Association.

Just having the recorded materials available to a class or to later historians is valuable in itself, but the tape will be much more accessible if you go one step further and at least provide an index. Future historians will be very reluctant to listen to six or more hours of tape in order to retrieve one specific anecdote, easily mentioned in an index. Even for one's own family, you may have ten hours of tape on your grandmother, but when your family gathers for a reunion you can pull out one-half hour's worth of anecdotes if your index is well done.

When transcribing tapes for historical purposes, be very careful. Naturally, every transcriber will try to make as accurate a typed report as possible. However, precise transcription is of the utmost importance when the oral history interview will be used for publication. Every name, location, and event should be checked for correct spelling, Inaudible or garbled phrases should be replayed many times and listened to by other transcribers in order to decipher the words. And the interviewee should be given an opportunity to see and correct the transcript before it reaches its final form. For more information on how to transcribe material, see chapter 8.

A class may decide to enlarge the oral history project. Here are some suggestions to expand the impact of interviews:

• BOOKS on the history of a specific region or ethnic group, for example, *By Myself I'm a Book,* a history of early Jewish immigration to Pittsburgh.

• A series of NEWSPAPER ARTICLES on local history featuring persons who have been interviewed by the group.

• LECTURES to the community on the history of their city.

• PRESENTATION to parents about the history the class uncovered.

• A FAIR including people and the crafts they described or featuring students re-creating old-fashioned crafts.

Oral history in the classroom can involve simulated interviews to make history come alive. In one Sunday school class, the teacher asked students to read a portion of the book of Exodus. Each was then instructed to conduct an interview with Moses as he received the Ten Commandments. This technique can be used for any historical figure or for characters in literature. In this way, oral history opens a pathway which helps young people become actively involved in understanding the past.

10
Legal Forms

The signing of legal forms may come as an unpleasant surprise to family members or others close to you. The object of having several types of legal forms for oral history is to protect both the interviewer and the interviewee. If the interviewer is considering writing a book based on the taped interviews or making the tapes public, then he needs to make sure he has the narrator's approval. The interviewee may want only a specific section of the tapes made available or may request a delay in their release. These restrictions are known within the profession as "closing" the tapes. For either of these situations, it is important to have a legal understanding between the interviewer and the person interviewed.

There is no reason to use formal language in order to have a binding agreement. It is best to write a simple and clear statement. We recommend that you tailor your own agreements to suit the interviewing circumstances: family, organization, business or community. There are several kinds of forms whch may be written quite informally and still have binding force:
- the pre-recording understanding
- the agreement on use or release form
- the limitation on publication

Here are some ways in which the statements might be phrased:

The Pre-recording Understanding
This can be a simple letter (with two copies, one for you and one for the narrator) that explains what you are planning to do,

why you want a recording of the interviewee's life experiences, and how you plan to tape the interview.

Sample Letter

Dear _____

As I explained to you on the phone (or by previous letter), I would like to make a tape recording of your reminiscences about your life (your business experiences, your involvement in certain issues) to pass on to my children to preserve as an historical record. The recording will take place in one or two sessions at any location that you choose. I (or one of the class or staff members) will do the recording and I'll give you a final copy of any resulting tapes or transcripts if you would like them. Please sign this letter and return it to me so that I know you understand why I want to interview you.
(Enclose self-addressed, stamped envelope).

Naturally, this letter should be signed before any interview is conducted. However, after the interview is completed, you will need to have the agreement on use verified.

Agreement on Use

For a family oral history project, the agreement on use can be kept quite informal. You don't want to intimidate your relative and scare him or her into thinking he/she is signing away important rights. Therefore, a one line statement may be all you need (two copies).

Sample Agreement (For Family Interviews)

I, _____ , give permission to _____ the interviewer, to use these tapes for family purposes.
/s/date

If your intention to use the tapes goes beyond passing them down for family history, add other sentences such as:

If the interviewer wishes to use any portion of the tapes for publication, he will inform me first, if at all possible. In the event of my death, any portion of the tapes may be published.

102

The simple agreement on use for family purposes may need to be changed slightly if you are conducting the interview for business or community history. Then you might wish to have the agreement, like the pre-recording understanding, signed in advance. That way there will be little chance of confusion or misunderstanding about what will be done with the tapes and/or transcripts. An amended form of the agreement on use for non-family purposes might read:

Sample Agreement (For Non-Family Interviews)

I, _____ , give permission to _____ [person, organization] to use any tapes and transcripts from this interview for historical, scholarly, or educational purposes, including publication, lecture, slide show, or archival storage.

/s/date

Some interviewees may wish to limit the use of their tapes only to certain people or to certain portions of the recording. In this case, you can add sentences (or clauses) which will enumerate which parts of the tape are "closed," for how long, or to which specific people. Those clauses can be written into the agreement on use and phrased in any way you and the narrator desire. Some samples of possible clauses are:

Sample Limitations on Use

- These tapes and/or transcripts are to be closed until ten (twenty) years after my death.
- Only the first half-hour of tape may be used for publication purposes.
- These tapes may be used only by scholars researching the history of the _____.
- The portion of tape (volume two, side two, time-segment fifteen minutes-twenty-five minutes) and/or transcripts pertaining to my involvement in government policy formulation are to be closed until my death or that of my wife (youngest child, etc.)

103

- These tapes are to be closed until all participants named in the interview have died.

The final clause is one you should try to avoid since it obviously will be extremely difficult to verify the deaths of all people mentioned on tape. However, if the interviewee is of great historical significance, it may be worthwhile to have the tapes no matter what the limitations.

The object of the legal forms is to allow as broad a use as possible for the tapes and/or transcripts. But if the interviewee balks at such a limitless release of his oral history record, any pre-arranged limitations may be written into the agreement on use. Whenever limitations on use are made, be sure they are adhered to by future listeners. Place a copy of the limitation securely on the outside of the cassettes and be especially careful about tape storage. It is best, as mentioned before, to place tapes of historical importance in a library or historical society.

Tape Recording Terms

AUTOMATIC SHUT-OFF: A special switch incorporated in some tape recorders which automatically turns off the machine when the tape ends.

AVC: Stands for automatic volume control. Newer machines will record at a constant level. However, if you are recording on an older model and you stop to check your tape and find no sound is being recorded, you should check to see if the volume control is turned to the lowest possible position. Older machines require that you manually set the volume control.

BIAS: A signal added intentionally during recording to avoid or neutralize the inherent non-linearity of magnetic systems. For purposes of oral history interviews, you can purchase a tape with either high or low bias. For voice only, it does not matter which you choose.

BULK ERASER: A device used to erase an entire cassette tape.

CAPSTAN: The spindle or shaft in a tape recorder which rotates against the tape pulling it through the machine at a constant speed.

DEMAGNETIZER: A device used to neutralize magnetic particles left as residue on the head of the machine. Demagnetizing the heads after every 20 hours of playing/recording time with a demagnetizer will create a clearer tape.

DUB: A copy of another recording. Cassette tapes are easily duplicated but the copy should always be made from the original as each successive copy loses some of its clarity.

EDITING: The selective correction of a tape recording by physically eliminating or replacing unwanted sections of the tape. This can be done two ways: by re-recording over the unwanted section or by cutting out the actual tape and splicing the two new ends together.

ERASURE: A means of removing recorded sound from the tape. An "erase" head on a machine automatically removes the unwanted sections simply by pressing the button. A magnet can be used to erase a tape, but some residual noise may remain.

FAST FORWARD: The button on the tape recorder which allows tape to run rapidly through the machine.

HEAD: The electromagnet across which the tape is drawn. This can be seen on the machine when you pop open the little plastic door which houses the cassette. When cleaning the head, disconnect the power source and depress the play button to make the head easily visible. The purpose of the head is to erase a previous recording, record, or play the tape. Most inexpensive machines have a separate erase head but only one combination record/playback head. Professional machines usually have three separate heads, one for each of these functions.

IMPEDANCE: Describes the input and output connections on a tape recorder which must be properly matched when connecting another electronic device such as a microphone or another tape recorder. A mismatch will produce power loss or frequency incompatibility. To avoid problems, check with a technical expert.

INPUT JACK: The terminal on the side or front of the machine where another electronic component can be attached.

IPS: Abbreviation for the tape speed which is given in "inches-per-second".

JACK: The receptacle for a plug on a tape recorder.

LAVALIER MICROPHONE: Individual microphone which is attached to your shirt or jacket. Similar to the mikes used in television interviews. These mikes require batteries and a special cord called a Y Cord.

LEVEL INDICATOR: A feature on some tape recorders which indicates the volume level at which the recording is being made. The needle will be bouncing to indicate that your voice is recording. Sometimes called a VU meter.

LOW NOISE TAPE: Magnetic tape produced without audible background noise (hiss) and without loss of fidelity.

MAGNETIC TAPE: Plastic tape which has been coated with a layer of magnetizable iron oxide particles. The result is a tape used for recording which can be easily erased and re-used.

MICROPHONE: A device for converting sound waves into electrical energy. Some recorders have a built-in mike; others require an external mike to be plugged into the machine.

MONITOR HEAD: Separate playback head in some tape recorders which makes it possible to listen to the recorded material instantly after the recording is made.

PATCH CORD: A short cord or cable with a plug on either end which allows two pieces of sound equipment to be connected electronically, i.e., one tape recorder to another, a phonograph to a tape recorder, an amplifier to a speaker, etc.

PAUSE CONTROL: A feature on some tape recorders which makes it possible to temporarily stop the machine without using the play/record buttons. No slag will be audible on the tape. Pause control is a particularly convenient feature for those doing many oral history interviews.

PINCH ROLLER: A spring-loaded rubber wheel in the tape recorder which holds the magnetic tape tightly against the capstan which then permits the tape to pass over the heads at a constant speed. You can see the pinch roller only when the plastic cassette door is open.

POWER CORD: The cord used to connect the tape recorder to an external power source. It is best to purchase a machine which comes with a power cord so you do not have to rely on batteries.

REWIND BUTTON: The lever used to rapidly rewind the tape.

SPLICING BLOCK: A metal or plastic device with a groove in it where a tape is placed when it needs to be spliced. This may be helpful but you can splice on any hard surface.

SPLICING TAPE: A pressure-sensitive, non-magnetic tape used to join together two ends of magnetic tape. Can be used if some material has been deliberately cut out of the tape or if the tape is broken and needs repair.

TAKE-UP REEL: The reel on the cassette which accumulates the tape as it is played through the machine.

TAPE LIFTERS: Movable guides which lift the tape from contact with the recording heads during fast forward or fast rewinding modes.

TAPE PLAYER: A unit capable only of playing pre-recorded tapes. Does not have a recording head and hence cannot be used for conducting interviews. This is what most of the "walkman" type machines are. For oral history purposes, you will need a tape recorder.

TAPE SPLICER: A mechanism used for splicing magnetic tape. Many different models exist.

TELEPHONE PICK-UP: This inexpensive device is a suction cup which you place on the ear piece of the handset of your telephone. Its other end is a jack which you place directly into your tape recorder. If you are unable to interview face-to-face and wish to do a long distance interview, the telephone pick-up is particularly useful.

TONE CONTROL: A knob on the recorder used to vary the base and treble sounds. Often used in the playback mode to balance the sound.

VU METER: A "volume unit" meter which monitors recording levels. It is found in high quality machines.

Index

AC adapter cord, 42
Agreement on use
   family interview, 101–2
   nonfamily interview, 103–4
Approval (legal), 101–4

Background information, 29ff
Batteries, 49, 55
Battery indicator, 43
Binding of transcript, 81
Birth certificates, 30
Business history, 62, 103

Cassettes, 47–49, 54, 60
   See also Tape recordings and
    Tape Recorders
Classroom projects, 87ff
Classroom projects
   publication, 93
   tape uses, 93
   topics, 94–95
Closed questions
   compared with open-ended,
    19ff, 59

"Closing" option, 103
   sample phrasing, 103–4
Columbia University Oral History
   Research Office, 89
Comments, bracketed, 72
Commercial transcripts, 67ff
Community historical projects,
   87ff, 103
   index of tape, 61–65, 98
   rights and responsibilities, 93
   tape storage, 97
   topics, 94–95
Composite Portrait, 16
Confidentiality, 103

Death certificates, 30
Demagnetizer, 44
Dictating machine, 68
Digital tape counter, 43, 62
Divorce records, 30

Earphones, 44
Editing, 69–79
Editing privileges, 103

Equipment. *See* Cassettes, Tape recordings, and Video cameras
Erasures, 48–49, 60, 67
Extension cords, 49
Extraneous comments, 55, 76–78

Family oral history, 1–9
  importance of index, 61–65
  sample questionnaires, 29ff
Famous people,
  editing and "closing," 103
  indexing of tape, 61–65
  and legal approval, 101–4
  tape storage, 48, 97, 104
Fiduciary relationships, 91
Foot-pedal, 43
Foxfire project, 89

Genealogy, 1
Glossary, 65–66
Government Printing Office booklet, 30
Guidelines, 90ff
Grandparents, 3, 13

Haley, Alex, 13
Headphone set, 44
"High-fidelity" tape, 47

Immigrant family histories, 34–35
  foreign terms, 65–66
  interview sample, 34–35
  questioning techniques, 20
Index preparation, 61–65
  community project, 62
  indexable items, 62
  time-segment system, 63–64
Inteviewee. *See* Narrator

Interviewer,
  extraneous comments of, 55, 76–78
  guidelines for, 17, 18, 90ff
  responsibility, 90ff
  See also Editing, Interviews, Transcript preparation
Interviews, 54ff
  advance data gathering, 32ff
  beginning and setting-up, 51–54
  interviewer/narrator selection, 11ff, 17
  preparation, 32ff
  supplies needed, 49
Introduction, 54

Legal forms and phrases, 101–4
Legal rights, 91ff, 101–4
Limitations on use, 103ff
Literary rights, 92

Magnetic tape, 48–49
  magnetism and erasures, 48–49, 67
  maintenance, 48
  recommended, 47
  storage of, 48
Marriage certificates, 30
Microphones, 42–43, 54
  dummy plug, 43
  on-off switch, 58, 68
"Mike-fright," 55

Narrator
  background research on, 29ff
  communicating with, 17–18, 29–32
  guidelines for, 14
  legal protection, 101–4

selection of, 14
storytelling ability, 14ff, 24–25
taping session, 51ff
transcript correction, 67–68
Nevins, Allan, 88
Noise interference, 52–53
Nonimmigrant family histories
  interview sample, 35
  questioning techniques, 19ff
Note-taking, 57, 60

"Off-the-record" remarks, 58
Open-ended questions,
  compared with closed, 19ff
Oral History Association, 90
Oral history programs, schools
  and universities, 89
  guidelines and responsibilities,
    91ff. *See also* Classroom proj-
    ects
Outlines,
  family history sample, 36ff
  future indexing, 62–64
  immigrant sample, 34–35
  nonimmigrant sample, 35

Pause control, 43
Photographs, 80, 81
Pre-recording understanding,
  90–93, 101–4
Pronunciation guide, 65–66
Publication, 67–81
  limitations, 103–4

Questionnaires, 34ff
Questions
  background, 29ff
  closed and open-ended, 19ff
  about family, 32ff
  inclusion in transcripts, 73ff

technique for asking, 19ff, 25,
  54ff

Recording. *See* Tape recordings
Release forms, 93, 97–98, 101–4
Relatives, 1–9
  deceased, 16
  selection of, 14ff, 24–25
  See also Family oral history
Re-recording, 48–49, 60, 67
Reversing switch, 43
Rights, 91–92, 101–4
Royalties, 91

School projects. *See* Classroom
  projects
Seal privileges, 91
Splicer, 48
Storage of tapes, 48–49, 60
Students and teachers, 87ff
Switches, 42–43, 62, 68

Table of contents, 79–80
Tape recordings
  erasures, 48
  indexing of, 61–65
  labeling of, 60
  noise interference, 52–53
  See also Cassettes, Editing, In-
    terviews, Magnetic tape,
    Transcripts
Tape tabs, 48, 67
Tape. *See* Magnetic tape
Taping session. *See* Interviews
Telephone pickup device, 17
Time-segment outline, 63–64
Topics, community and school,
  94–95
Transcribing, 67–81
  commercial services, 67–68

113

of community projects, 87ff
editing of, 69ff
legal release, 79
machines to aid preparation of,
  67–68

Video Cameras, 45–47

Watch, use of, 49
Written record. *See* Transcribing
Wigginton, Eliot, 89